Oracle Certification Prep

Study Guide for

1Z0-497: Oracle Database 12c Essentials

Matthew Morris

Study Guide for Oracle Database 12c Essentials (Exam 1Z0-497) Rev 1.0

ISBN-13: 978-1-941404-00-3
ISBN-10: 1941404006

Table of Contents

What to expect from the test 8

What to Expect from this Study Guide 9

Additional Study Resources 10

Oracle Database Software 11

Describe the key characteristics of a relational database 11

Summarize locking behavior in an Oracle database 14

Describe the differences between data concurrency and data consistency 16

Describe the various steps of a database transaction 18

Administration & Configuration 21

Design a database, identify requirements, create the logical design and physical database design 21

Install and configure a database 24

Grant Enterprise Manager administrative privileges 28

Use SQL*Plus and SQL Developer to access your database 31

Oracle Database 12c New Features 35

Setup a Global Database Service (GDS) 35

Define declarative policies for Oracle Data Redaction 37

Apply best practices for running the ADDM Advisor 41

Maximum Availability Architecture 47

Implement the various replication options available to the Oracle database 47

Explain the architectural differences between Data Guard and Active Data Guard 50

Implement the various Data Guard configurations available 51
Create an MAA architecture that leverages Active Data Guard and Oracle Golden Gate 56
Choose the appropriate high availability architecture based on various planned and unplanned scenarios 57
Backup and Recovery 63
Explain general best practices and guidelines for backups on the Oracle database 63
Implement recovery procedures for various failure scenarios 69
Use the Data Recovery Advisor for backup and recovery solutions 73
Monitoring 78
Use Oracle Enterprise Manager to view database storage structures ..78
Apply different strategies for interacting with the database using SQL Developer 81
Describe the EM Cloud Control and EM Express architecture as it relates to the database 85
Manage structures used to undo changes made to the database and maintain data consistency 89
Administering Users and Security 94
Create and administer users 94
Grant privileges to users to perform database operations...................98
Create and manage roles 103
Software Installation and Maintenance..106
Install the Oracle database software 106
Locate patches for the Oracle database 114
Apply best practices to patching the database 115
Apply troubleshooting tasks for planned database maintenance 119

View and modify the parameters used to configure the Oracle instance 121
Oracle Data Structures......129
Articulate the various schema objects in a relational database 129
Perform different index scans and relate them to index types 131
Leverage partitioning in an Oracle database 137
Use the data dictionary and the dynamic performance views 140
Identify the various tools for data movement and analysis 143
Oracle Database Instance Architecture 154
Define the main components of an Oracle Instance 154
Describe the various stages of a database instance 155
Articulate the various basic memory structures......162
Describe how a block of data is written to the database 164
Articulate the mandatory background processes......167
Oracle Multitenant Architecture 172
Create a pluggable database (PDB)......173
Articulate the difference between a Container database and a Pluggable database......175
Perform administration tasks on a container database (CDB)......176
Manage processes in a CDB 181
Manage physical and logical structures in a CDB......181
Describe the various storage options for a PDB 182
Oracle Network Architecture......183
Describe the Oracle Database listener architecture......184
Configure and connect to a database service......185
Configure a database listener 187

What to expect from the test

The test consists of 85 multiple choice or multiple answer questions and you have 120 minutes to complete it. The passing score listed on Oracle Education at this time is 70%, but as with all Oracle certification tests, they note it is subject to change. For multiple-answer questions, you must provide all of the correct answers to get credit for the question. Answer every question on the exam – an unanswered question counts off the same amount as an incorrect one.

The 12c Essentials exam covers a fairly broad range of topics both in terms of what they are about and their relative complexity. Many of the topics are basic associate-level tasks such as understanding RDBMS theory, creating users, and knowing the difference between an instance and a database. Others topics are on relatively high-level subjects such as Data Guard, Global Database Services, and Oracle GoldenGate. Oracle University has geared this exam towards testing to ensure that candidates have a broad but shallow level of knowledge across a large number of topics. You will not need to know the specifics of installing Oracle Data Guard, or GoldenGate, or Global Database Services. However, you must understand what they are, how they can be used in the real world, and what problems they were designed to solve. For the more common associate-level information, you will be required to know more specifics.

A fair number of the questions on the exam were what Oracle University calls 'Learner-Level'. If you have done much preparation on the topics, these are the ones that you immediately answer and feel good about. However, a number of questions went considerably deeper or into greater detail than I really thought would be (possibly should be) the case for this exam. Do not assume that because this is an 'Implementation' exam that all of the questions are going to involve rote memorization. However, there were no true 'Scenario-based' questions and the exam contained absolutely no exhibits. I would put the difficulty level just over that of an OCA-level certification exam.

What to Expect from this Study Guide

This document is built around the subject matter topics that Oracle Education has indicated will be tested. This book contains material from several Oracle documentation sources including both the 12c manuals and whitepapers published by Oracle. The guide covers a significant percentage of the information and operations that you must be familiar with in order to pass the exam.

What this guide is intended to do is to present the information that will be covered on the exam at the level it will likely be asked. Unless you have experience with the Oracle database, I highly recommend that you combine this study guide with some hands-on practice installing and using the Oracle database. You can download both the software and the manuals from Oracle's website. Many of the features covered in this exam only exist in the Enterprise version of Oracle, so even if you have hands-on experience with Oracle XE, it may well not be applicable to the exam.

The goal of this guide is to present to you the concepts and information most likely to be the subject of test questions, and to do so in a very compact format that will allow you to read through it more than once to reinforce the information. The companion website mentioned on the next page has links to all of the resources I used in researching for this guide. I highly recommend making use of those resources to gain further insight into the topics of this exam. While I have tried to distill the most critical information from those sources, reading the original material may help you to gain a better understanding of the various topics. That will not only improve your chances of passing the exam but make it more likely that this information in this exam will prove useful to you in your career.

Additional Study Resources

The companion website to this series is www.oraclecertificationprep.com. The site contains many additional resources that can be used to study for this exam (and others). From the entry page of the website, click on the 'Exams' button, and then select the link for this test. The Exam Details page contains links to the following information sources:

- Applicable Oracle documentation.
- Third-party books relevant to the exam.
- White papers and articles on Oracle Learning Library on topics covered in the exam.
- Articles on the Web that may be useful for the exam.
- Videos at YouTube and other sites that provide relevant tutorials.

The website will never link to unauthorized content such as brain dumps or illegal content such as copyrighted material made available without the consent of the author. I cannot guarantee the accuracy of the content links. While I have located the data and scanned it to ensure that it is relevant to the given exam, I have not proofread it. The material on the Oracle Learning Library is almost certain to be completely accurate and most of the other links come from highly popular Oracle support websites and are created by experienced Oracle professionals.

I recommend that you use more than one source of study materials whenever you are preparing for a certification. Reading information presented from multiple different viewpoints can help to give you a more complete picture of any given topic. The links on the website can help you to do this. Fully understanding the information covered in this certification is not just valuable so that getting a passing score is more likely – it will also help you in your career. I guarantee that in the long run, any knowledge you gain while studying for this certification will provide more benefit to you than any piece of paper or line on your resume.

Oracle Database Software

Describe the key characteristics of a relational database

Databases, regardless of the specific format or implementation used, provide a means for organizations to store and retrieve information. Any given set of components and processes for collecting, storing, and retrieving information is effectively a database. Mind you, by this definition, a filing cabinet is a database. Information to be stored is placed into a folder in one of the cabinet drawers. Each drawer and their contents are sorted based on some aspect of the data being stored (generally alphabetically, numerically, or chronologically). If there is a need to access the information at a future date, this sorting allows for the record to be located rapidly.

Once computers began to have the storage capacity and computing power required to hold and process significant quantities of information, the first Database Management Systems (DBMS) were developed. A DBMS facilitates the operations required to store, organize, and retrieve information in a database. There are several different logical models around which a database management system can be designed. The models dictate how information is organized in the files used by the management system. The data organization has implications on the flexibility and performance of the database application. Some of the database models include:

- **Flat** -- Flat file databases are the simplest model there is. They have very little flexibility, consisting of only two dimensions (rows and columns). They cannot contain complex data relationships. However, they are still commonly used as a means for transferring data between systems. Delimited or fixed-width text files are effectively flat-file databases and almost every DBMS has the ability to read and import data from them.
- **Hierarchical** -- In this model, the data is organized into a tree-like structure. Information can be represented using parent/child relationships: each parent can have many children, but each child

has only one parent. This is also known as a one-to-many relationship.

- **Network** -- As with the hierarchical database model, the network model structures data as a tree of records. However, while the hierarchical model allows each child only one parent, the network model allows each record to have multiple parent and child records, forming a generalized graph structure
- **Relational** -- The relational model is based on first-order predicate logic. In the relational model, all data is represented in terms of tuples, grouped into relations.

Regardless of the data model, a database management system typically consists of the following elements:

- **Kernel code** -- The kernel manages memory and storage for the DBMS.
- **Metadata Repository** -- The repository contains information about the data being stored and is generally called the data dictionary.
- **Query language** -- The query language provides the interface by which applications can store, update, and retrieve data.

E. F. Codd defined a relational model based on mathematical set theory in 1970. Databases designed around the relational model are the most widely used today. Prior to the relational model, data was stored in rigid relationships that could not be modified easily using a Data Definition Language (DDL). The relational model provides a structure for a logical view of the data to be stored. It uses a number of mathematical constructs for this: domains, relations, tuples, and attributes. Each of these constructs have names that are used in databases. Domains for example define the data type being stored (i.e. character, number, date). In addition to the data structure, the relational model defines how data will be manipulated using relational algebra. It also defines the means for specifying and enforcing data integrity.

Codd's paper was essentially a mathematical exercise and used several terms that really only matter when you are performing relational algebra. In eighteen years working with RDBMS's, I have never found a need to use relational algebra. However, you may see some of the terms used in relational theory for the exam:

- **Tuple** -- Row
- **Relation** – A set of tuples.
- **Attribute** – Column
- **Attribute Value** – Column value
- **Domain** – Column data type
- **Entity** – Table

The physical data stored in an RDBMS is independent from the logical data structures designed to represent it. Oracle stores the logical data structures in a database schema. A schema is a collection of logical data structures which are also referred to as schema objects. Each schema is owned by and has the same name as a database user. Schema objects refer to the data in the database and are created by the user via Data Definition Language. Two of the more important schema objects are tables and indexes:

- **Table** -- Used to store the information, tables are defined with a name and a one or more columns. Each column in a table has a name and data type. Columns may also be defined with a maximum size and rules (known as integrity constraints) that determine whether or not data can be entered into them.
- **Index** -- Can optionally be created against one or more columns of a table. Indexes can be used to speed up access when querying a table. Unique indexes can also be used to ensure that no duplicate data is entered into a table.

Structured Query Language (SQL) is the ANSI standard language for relational databases. SQL is a set-based declarative language. It is a nonprocedural language that allows users to specify a desired result rather than the actions required to achieve that result. Using SQL, a user can select all rows from a given table and the RDBMS will determine the exact steps required in order to retrieve and display the results. SQL statements enable you to perform the following tasks:

- Query the database
- Insert, update, and delete rows in a table
- Create, replace, alter, and drop objects
- Control access to the database and its objects
- Guarantee database consistency and integrity

Summarize locking behavior in an Oracle database

Locks are mechanisms that prevent destructive interaction between transactions accessing the same resource. Some of the resources that Oracle locks are user objects, such as tables and rows. There are also locks against system objects such as shared data structures in memory and data dictionary rows. There are three broad classes of locks (listed below). For the purposes of this exam, we'll deal only with DML locks.

- **DML Locks** – Protect data. For example, table locks lock entire tables, while row locks lock selected rows.
- **DDL Locks** – Protect the structure of schema objects—for example, the dictionary definitions of tables and views.
- **System Locks** – Protect internal database structures such as data files. Latches, mutexes, and internal locks are entirely automatic.

As a general rule, there is no user-interaction in obtaining locks. When executing SQL, Oracle automatically determines what locks are required and obtains them. However, Oracle provides the capability to manually obtain locks on user objects.

A transaction might lock a single row, multiple rows, or an entire table. When obtaining locks automatically, Oracle will always choose the lowest-level of locking possible. Also, locks in Oracle do not escalate. Some databases will 'escalate' row level locking to a table lock once a certain number or percentage of rows in a table are locked. This behavior will never happen in Oracle. Once one session obtains a lock on a particular resource, no other session may modify that resource until the transaction holding the lock has completed. However, the resource is still available for read operations. Query operations never obtain a lock and are not blocked by existing locks.

A DML lock, or data lock, guarantees the integrity of table data accessed concurrently by multiple users. DML locks prevent destructive interference of simultaneous conflicting DML or DDL operations. When issuing a DML statement, Oracle will automatically acquire a row lock and a table lock:

Row Locks (TX)

A row lock, also called a TX lock, is obtained for a single row of a table. A transaction will require a row lock for every row that is being modified. The row lock exists until the transaction commits or rolls back. These locks act to queue transactions so that no two transactions modify the same row at the same time. Oracle will always lock a modified row in exclusive mode and other transactions cannot modify that row until the first transaction ends. Row locking provides the highest possible concurrency. Oracle stores lock information in the data block that contains the locked row.

Table Locks (TM)

A table lock, also called a TM lock, is acquired by a transaction when a table is modified by a DML statement. DML operations require table locks to reserve DML access to the table on behalf of a transaction and to prevent conflicting DDL operations (for example a DDL operation that drops a column which contains data being updated by a DML operation). Table locks come in the following modes:

- **Row Share (RS)** – This class of lock, also called a subshare table lock (SS), indicates that the transaction holding the lock on the table has locked rows in the table and intends to update them. A row share lock is the least restrictive mode of table lock, offering the highest degree of concurrency for a table.
- **Row Exclusive Table Lock (RX)** – This lock, also called a subexclusive table lock (SX), generally indicates that the transaction holding the lock has updated table rows or issued SELECT ... FOR UPDATE. An SX lock allows other transactions to query, insert, update, delete, or lock rows concurrently in the same table. Therefore, SX locks allow multiple transactions to

obtain simultaneous SX and subshare table locks for the same table.

- **Share Table Lock (S)** – A share table lock held by a transaction allows other transactions to query the table (without using SELECT ... FOR UPDATE), but updates are allowed only if a single transaction holds the share table lock. Because multiple transactions may hold a share table lock concurrently, holding this lock is not sufficient to ensure that a transaction can modify the table.
- **Share Row Exclusive Table Lock (SRX)** – This lock, also called a share-subexclusive table lock (SSX), is more restrictive than a share table lock. Only one transaction at a time can acquire an SSX lock on a given table. An SSX lock held by a transaction allows other transactions to query the table (except for SELECT ... FOR UPDATE) but not to update the table.
- **Exclusive Table Lock (X)** – This lock is the most restrictive, prohibiting other transactions from performing any type of DML statement or placing any type of lock on the table.

Describe the differences between data concurrency and data consistency

Any multiuser DBMS must be able to handle concurrency. Concurrency is the simultaneous access of the same data by multiple users. In a database without concurrency controls, users could make changes to data that would compromise data integrity. For example, if two users were to simultaneously update the same row, the end results would be indeterminate.

The most common method for handling concurrency in a multi-user environment when more than one user tries to modify the same data is to make all but one of the users wait. From a performance and usability standpoint, however, the ideal is to make that wait time either nonexistent or negligible. The goal is for SQL statements that modify data to proceed with minimal interference from the database. Oracle uses locks to control concurrent access to data. Locking provides a mechanism that prevents one transaction from acting destructively on a second transaction accessing a shared resource. Locks help ensure data integrity while allowing maximum concurrent availability to the data.

A closely related concept to concurrency is data consistency. Data consistency means that each user in the database must see a consistent view of the data. For a given user, the view of the data will include uncommitted changes made by their own transactions plus any committed transactions made by other users.

The database must prevent what are called 'dirty reads'. This occurs when one transaction sees uncommitted changes made by a concurrent transaction in a different user's session. Oracle enforces statement-level read consistency. This guarantees that data returned by a query is always committed and consistent with respect to a single point in time. This point may be the time at which the statement was opened or the time at which the transaction began. For example, if a long running SQL statement is executed, the data returned will always be what existed when the query was first executed, even if it has changed before the query ends. It is also possible for Oracle to provide read consistency to all queries in a transaction. This is transaction-level read consistency and ensures each statement in a transaction sees data from the time at which the transaction began.

All Oracle transactions comply with the basic properties of a database transaction, known as ACID properties. ACID is an acronym for the following:

- **Atomicity** – All tasks of a transaction are performed or none of them are. There are no partial transactions.
- **Consistency** – The transaction takes the database from one consistent state to another consistent state.
- **Isolation** – The effect of a transaction is not visible to other transactions until the transaction is committed.
- **Durability** – Changes made by committed transactions are permanent. After a transaction completes, the database ensures through its recovery mechanisms that changes from the transaction are not lost.

Describe the various steps of a database transaction

A transaction starts when an executable SQL statement is processed by the database. This can be any SQL statement that generates a call to the database instance, including DML and DDL statements or the SET TRANSACTION statement.

Once a transaction begins, it will be assigned to an available undo data segment. This segment will be used to record the undo entries for the transaction. When the first DML statement is issued, an undo segment and transaction table slot are allocated and a transaction ID assigned. A transaction ID is unique to each transaction and represents the undo segment number, slot, and sequence number.

When a transaction has started but is not yet committed or rolled back, is it considered active. While the transaction remains active, all data changes made by it are temporary. They will not be made permanent until (and unless) the transaction is committed. Before the transaction ends, the state of the data is as follows:

- All rows affected by the data change are locked. While the transaction is active, other users cannot change the data in the affected rows, nor can they see the uncommitted changes.
- Undo information has been generated in the SGA. This data contains the values that existed prior to being altered by the SQL statements of the transaction.
- Redo data has been generated in the online redo log buffer of the SGA. Redo log records contain both changes to data blocks and changes to undo blocks.
- Changes have been made to the database buffers of the SGA. Any changes made to data blocks of a table will be made in memory first. Even after these changes have been committed, the altered blocks stored in the database buffers of the SGA are not necessarily written immediately to the data files. Oracle may perform the disk writes of these buffers before or after the commit.

An active transaction ends when any of the following occurs:

- A COMMIT or ROLLBACK statement without a SAVEPOINT clause is issued in the session. Once committed, changes made by the transaction are permanent and visible to other users.
- A DDL command is issued in the session. The database automatically issues an implicit COMMIT statement before and after every DDL statement. If there are any active transactions in the current session, Oracle commits the transaction and then runs and commits the DDL statement as a new, single-statement transaction.
- The user exits normally from the utility running the session. Most utilities and tools issue an implicit commit before exit by default, which will cause the current transaction to be committed.
- A client process terminates abnormally. Abnormal exits from a client utility will cause active transactions to be rolled back.

The following actions occur when a transaction commits:

- A System Change Number (SCN) will be generated for the COMMIT.
- The log writer (LGWR) process will write any remaining entries in the redo log buffers and the transaction SCN to the online redo log. This event constitutes the commit of the transaction.
- Any locks held on rows and tables are released.
- Any save points for the transaction are deleted.
- The database performs a commit cleanout. Oracle will remove lock-related transaction data from any blocks of the committed transaction that are still in the SGA, if no other session is modifying them.
- The transaction is marked complete and other users can view the changes.

Transaction control allows for the management of changes made by DML statements. There are three transaction control statements:

- **COMMIT** -- This statement ends the current transaction and makes all changes performed in the transaction permanent. It also erases all savepoints in the transaction and releases transaction locks.
- **ROLLBACK** -- This statement ends the current transaction and reverses all changes made by it. The ROLLBACK TO SAVEPOINT statement reverses all changes made since the last save point but does not end the entire transaction.
- **SAVEPOINT** -- This statement identifies a point in a transaction to which you can roll back without reversing changes made prior to the time the save point is issued.

Administration & Configuration

Design a database, identify requirements, create the logical design and physical database design

It is impossible to make informed decisions regarding database requirements without information. The first step in creating requirements then is to gather information about the company for which the database is being made. There are a number of potential sources for this data that are common to the majority of organizations. The most common sources for gathering information relevant to database development are interviews, business forms, and existing systems.

Interviews

Sit down for an interview with people in the organization who are currently performing the business processes that will be part of the database. They can assist in mapping the types of information they need, how that information flows through the organization, and what types of decisions they must make based on the data they have access to. Interviews are also a good way of determining what kind of data analysis is being done currently and shortcomings in the current process that could be resolved.

Business Forms

The forms used by an organization are an excellent way to get an ants-eye view of the data they utilize. These forms and documents can often be directly translated into tables required by the database. Some examples of business forms that can be useful include:

- Purchase orders
- Purchase requisitions
- Invoices
- Expense reports
- Shipping documents
- Timesheets
- Travel itineraries

Existing Systems

Very seldom will the need for a new database arise from a vacuum. The organization most likely already has another system in place where data is being stored. They may have outgrown the capabilities of the existing system or it no longer meets their requirements. The current system may not even be an actual database. As mentioned in the first topic of this guide, a filing cabinet is effectively a database. That might well be the 'current system' that must be replaced by an Oracle database. Often an organization will use spreadsheets to store information that ideally should be in a database. Whatever the organization is currently using to store and retrieve data, you should analyze it in order to determine its capabilities and shortcomings. Once you understand the current system, designing a replacement that will meet the requirements of the organization become much easier.

Ultimately the database design process should result in a system that satisfies the needs of the end users. However, users often are not able to identify what they need in the early stages of the design process. The most elegant database designs are designed with flexibility that will allow them to grow and change as the needs of the end users change.

Logical and Physical Design

Creating a logical model of a database prior to a physical one allows you to focus on the information requirements without having to immediately deal with implementation details. However, before beginning the logical design of a database, it is necessary that the following steps be performed:

- Define the business requirements.
- Determine the scope of the applications to be supported.
- Create a conceptual design of the database.

Until the above steps have been accomplished, there is nothing concrete on which to base decisions about what the logical design of the database should be. The logical design process is concerned with defining the objects that will be contained within the database and determine the relationships between them. It is a conceptual design that does not define any of the details involved in physically implementing the structures represented in the model.

During the logical design process, the data elements are arranged into a series of logical relationships called entities and attributes. An entity represents a chunk of information -- generally a table in relational databases. An attribute is a component of an entity. In relational databases, an attribute generally maps to a column. Logical designs can be created with anything from a white board drawing, to a spreadsheet, to purpose-built tools such as Oracle Warehouse Builder or Oracle Designer.

Entity-relationship diagrams are generally useful in mapping out the entities required for a database, their attributes, and how they relate to one another. This is logical design in a nutshell. Ideally, these entities and relationships should parallel operational data of the business subjects being modeled and the relationships between those subjects.

The completed logical design should define a set of objects and logical relationships among those objects. The physical design is the process of determining the most effective way for storing and retrieving those objects. In this stage you convert the information collected during the logical design phase into a description of the physical database, including tables and constraints. Decisions made during physical design, such as the number and types of indexes to use or the partitioning strategy to implement can have a significant impact on query performance.

In the physical design process, the logical model is translated into actual database structures. Some of the items that will be mapped include:

- Entities to Tables
- Relationships to Foreign Keys
- Attributes to Columns
- Primary Unique Identifiers to the Primary Key
- Unique Identifiers to Unique Keys

The structures where data will be stored are also determined during the physical design. These structures include:

- Data files
- Tablespaces
- Partitions
- Indexes

Install and configure a database

In the bad old days, creating a database meant building a CREATE DATABASE statement that did everything you wanted it to. No one misses those days. Oracle's Database Configuration Assistant (DBCA) is a much simpler means of creating a database. In addition, once DBCA has completed, the database is immediately ready to use. By contrast, a database generated with the CREATE DATABASE statement still requires several scripts to be run before the database can be used. DBCA can be launched directly from the Oracle Installer, or it can be launched as a standalone tool at any point after the Oracle software has been installed.

DBCA has two modes of operation: interactive mode or noninteractive/silent mode. The interactive mode makes use of a graphical user interface and guides you through creating and configuring a database. The noninteractive mode allows you to create the database via a script. DBCA is run in noninteractive mode by specifying command-line arguments, a response file, or both. This chapter will cover only the interactive mode.

To start DBCA, log on to your computer as a member of the group that is authorized to install Oracle and to create and run the database. To start DBCA on UNIX or Linux, or at the command-line prompt in Microsoft Windows, enter the following command: dbca. The dbca executable is located in the ORACLE_HOME/bin directory. Once started, the DBCA user interface guides you through a step-by-step process to create a database.

Step 1: Database Operation -- This screen allows you to create a database, configure or delete a database (grayed out in the screenshot below because no databases exist yet), manage templates for database creation, or manage pluggable databases (again grayed out because no CDB exists).

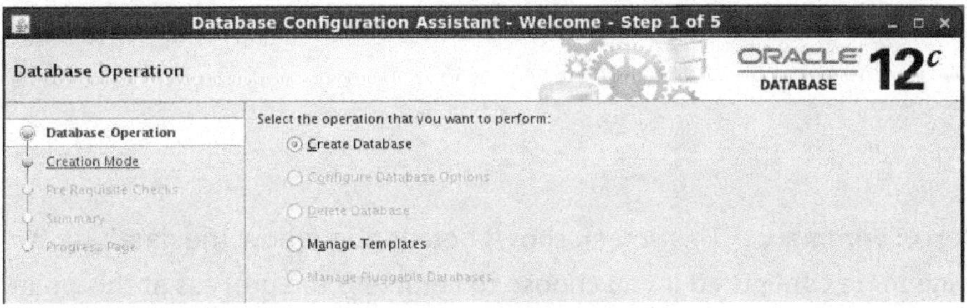

Step 2: Creation Mode -- In this step, you must choose the database name, storage type, location of the data files and fast recovery area, character set and the admin password. When using Oracle Enterprise Edition, you can also opt to create this as a container database. If you click the Advanced Mode radio button, you can customize some of the database parameters.

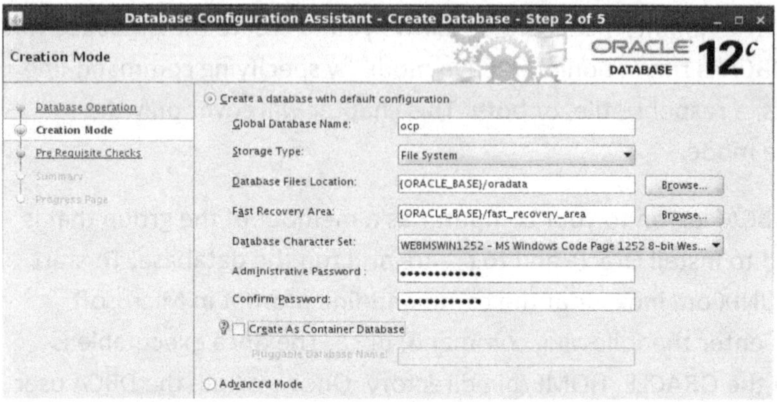

Step 3: Pre Requisite Checks -- DBCA verifies that all prerequisites have been met to create the database.

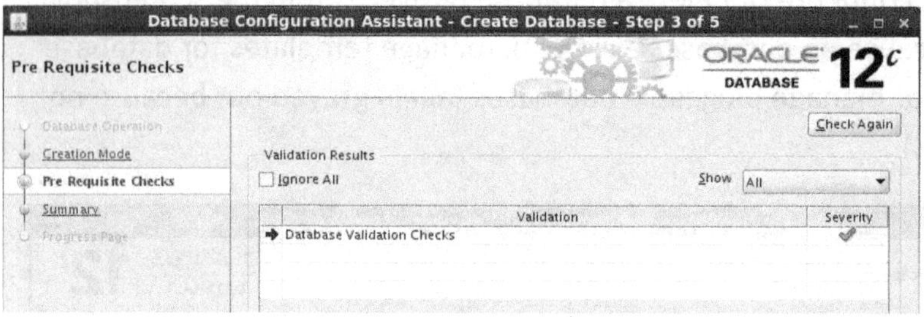

Step 4: Summary -- This screen shows details about how the database is going to be configured if you choose to complete the process at this point.

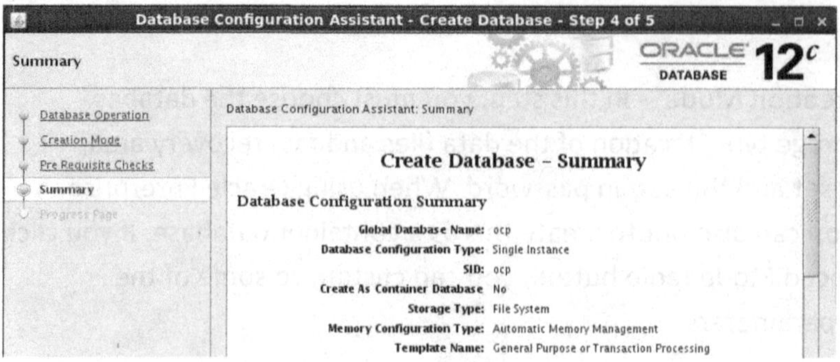

Step 5: Progress Page -- This screen allows you to follow the progress of DBCA as it builds the database.

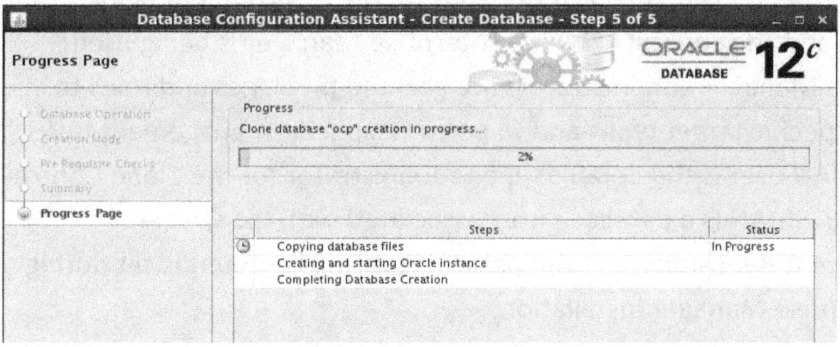

Once DBCA completes, the new database is started and ready to be used. You can connect to the database and begin creating users and objects immediately.

There are a number of environment variables associated with an Oracle installation. These should be set for operating system accounts that will be using the database.

- **ORACLE_BASE** – sets the base of the directory structure use for Optimal Flexible Architecture..
- **ORACLE_SID** – Sets the initial instance name used by the OS account.
- **ORACLE_HOME** – Specifies the directory where the Oracle software is installed.
- **NLS_LANG** – Specifies language, territory and character set settings.
- **TNS_ADMIN** -- Specifies the directory containing the Oracle Net Services configuration files.

Grant Enterprise Manager administrative privileges

There are several different classes of users supported in Oracle Enterprise Manager. The appropriate class depends on the environment being managed and the context in which Enterprise Manager is being used. Enterprise Manager administrators are granted privileges and roles to manage specific target types and to perform specific management tasks. The SYSMAN user is the default super administrator for the Cloud Control Console. SYSMAN is a database user associated with the Oracle Management Repository and the password for this account is set during the Enterprise Manager installation.

The Management Repository contains data that EM uses to assist in monitoring the performance and availability of the hardware and software you have deployed in an organization. The repository also contains information about EM administrators who have the privileges to access the data. It is possible to create and manage new Enterprise Manager administrator accounts. Each account will have its own login credentials, as well as an assigned set of roles and privileges. There are three administrator access categories:

- **Super Administrator** -- The highest class of Enterprise Manager administrator with full access privileges to all targets and administrator accounts within the Enterprise Manager environment. The SYSMAN Super Administrator is created by default when Enterprise Manager is installed. The SYSMAN account should only be used to perform infrequent system-wide, global configuration tasks. The Super Administrator can create other administrator accounts for routine administration tasks.
- **Administrator** -- This is a regular Enterprise Manager administrator.
- **Repository Owner** -- This account acts as the database administrator for the Management Repository and cannot be modified, duplicated, or deleted.

The management tasks which can be performed by a given administrator and the targets that can be accessed depend on the roles, system privileges, and target privileges that have been granted to the account. The Super Administrator can restrict certain administrators to perform only a given class of management tasks, or access a restricted set of targets, or to restrict both the management tasks and accessible targets.

A basic level of security in Enterprise Manager is determined by user privileges. User privileges control access to data and limit which SQL statements that can be executed. When creating a user, you grant privileges to enable the user to connect to the database, to run queries and make updates, to create schema objects, and more.

A role is a collection of Enterprise Manager resource privileges, target privileges, or both. Roles can be granted to administrators or to other roles. Roles allow for the grouping of privileges so that an administrator needs only to assign the role that includes all the appropriate privileges rather than having to grant each individual privileges. Roles facilitate dividing the administration workload among multiple administrators by filtering target access, or filtering access to management task, or both. Enterprise Manager 12c comes with a number of predefined roles to manage a wide variety of resource and target types. Some examples of the predefined roles are:

- **EM_ALL_ADMINISTRATOR** -- Role has privileges to perform Enterprise Manager administrative operations. It provides Full privileges on all secure resources (including targets)
- **EM_ALL_DESIGNER** -- Role has privileges to design Enterprise Manager operational entities such as Monitoring Templates.
- **EM_ALL_OPERATOR** -- Role has privileges to manage Enterprise Manager operations.
- **EM_ALL_VIEWER** -- Role has privileges to view Enterprise Manager operations.
- **EM_PATCH_ADMINISTRATOR** -- Role for creating, editing, deploying, deleting and granting privileges for any patch plan.
- **EM_USER** -- Role has privilege to access Enterprise Manager Application.

- **PUBLIC** – The public role is granted to all administrators. This role can be customized at the site level to group privileges that need to be granted to all administrators.

You can view the complete list of roles in the Oracle Enterprise Manager Cloud Control Administrator's Guide. The PUBLIC role automatically assigned to all new non-super administrators when they are created. By default it has no privileges assigned to it. The role should be used to define default privileges to be granted to non-super administrators.

A privilege is a right to perform management actions within Enterprise Manager. Enterprise Manager privileges are divided into two broad categories:

- **Target Privileges** -- These allow an administrator to perform operations on a target.
- **Resource Privileges** -- These privileges allow a user to perform operations against specific types of resources.

A subset of the available target and resource privileges follows. For the complete list, reference the Oracle Enterprise Manager Cloud Control Administrator's Guide.

Target Privileges:

- **FULL_ANY_TARGET** -- Ability to do all operations on all the targets, including delete the target
- **PERFORM_OPERATION_ANYWHERE** -- Execute any OS Command at any Agent
- **CONNECT_ANY_VIEW_TARGET** -- Ability to connect and manage any of the viewable target
- **EM_MONITOR** -- Ability to view any Enterprise Manager Repository targets
- **CREATE_TARGET** -- Ability to create a target
- **GROUP_ADMINISTRATION** -- Ability to administer groups

- **FULL_TARGET** -- Ability to do all operations on the target, including delete the target
- **CONFIGURE_TARGET** -- Ability to edit target properties

Resource Privileges:

- **Access Enterprise Manager** -- Ability to access Enterprise Manager interfaces
- **JVM Diagnostics User** -- Gives capability to view the JVM Diagnostic data
- **JVM Diagnostics Administrator** -- Gives capability to manage all JVM Diagnostic Administrative operations
- **Application Replay Operator** -- View, create, and edit any Application Replay entity.
- **Request Monitoring User** -- Gives capability to view the Request Monitoring Data
- **Manage change plans** -- Create and delete Change Manager change plans

Use SQL*Plus and SQL Developer to access your database

Oracle's SQL*Plus command line interface has existed essentially unchanged at least as far back as release 7 of Oracle. It is installed as a standard interface on all operating systems. From SQL*Plus you may submit and SQL to the database, execute stored SQL scripts, and spool output to files.

SQL*Plus is a very uncomplicated interface and is often used for troubleshooting problems when failures occur. When other interfaces cannot connect to the database, often SQL*Plus can still make a connection and allow administrators to diagnose a problem.The SQL*Plus interface is started by executing sqlplus at the command prompt of an OS terminal:

```
C:\> sqlplus
```

When sqlplus is executed with no parameters, it will prompt for the username and password of the Oracle account to connect to. Optionally, you can include the username and password separated by a slash (/). If applicable, you can provide a remote database name to connect to as well, for example:

```
C:\> sqlplus username/password@connect_identifier
```

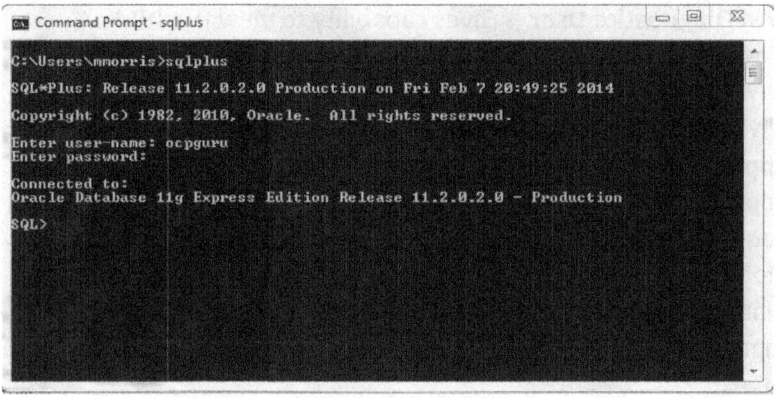

Executing the sqlplus command with the parameter /nolog will open a SQL*Plus window, but will not establish a connection to the database. Before issuing any SQL commands, you must issue a CONNECT command to establish a valid logon. Queries against the database will generate an error. It is possible to issue OS commands from SQL*Plus whether or not there is an active connection to the database by preceding the OS command with the 'host' keyword.

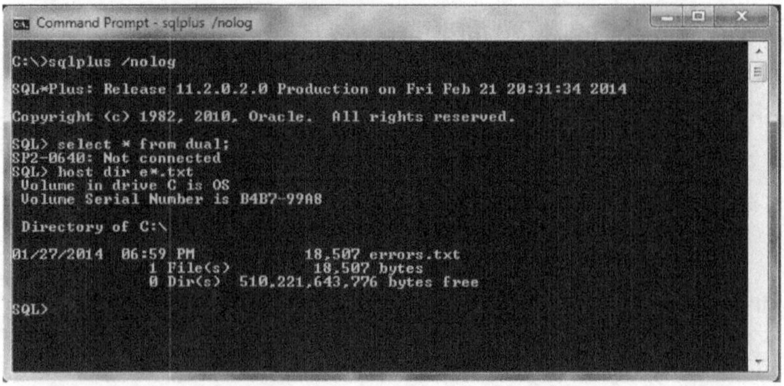

SQL Developer

When compared to SQL*Plus, the Oracle SQL Developer interface is a relatively new addition. It is a graphical user interface that provides functionality well beyond what is possible with SQL*Plus. The capabilities built into the interface are a significant subset of those available in fairly expensive third party interfaces such as Toad. SQL Developer allows users to browse database objects, run SQL statements, edit and debug PL/SQL statements and run reports.

SQL Developer is developed in Java and runs on Windows, Linux and the Mac OS X. It is possible to install SQL Developer on the database server and users can connect remotely from their desktops, to avoid client server network traffic. By default, connectivity to the database is provided through the JDBC Thin driver. SQL Developer can connect to Oracle Databases 9.2.0.1 and later for all Oracle database editions including Oracle XE.

As a GUI, SQL Developer is normally executed by clicking on an icon. Once the interface has initialized, normally the database connection is made by clicking on one of the available connections. For a new installation, it is necessary to create a new connection definition for the interface. If you have never used SQL Developer, there is a tutorial available on the Oracle Learning Library that will provide an introduction to using the tool.

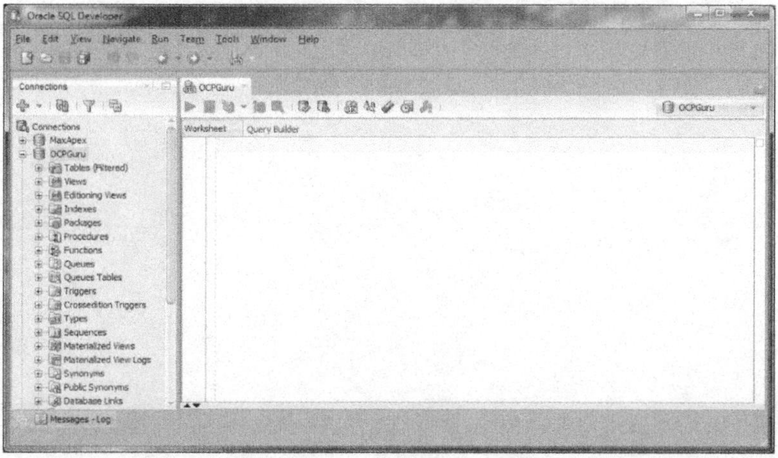

An interface to the Recovery Manager (RMAN) utility is built into SQL Developer. Recovery Manager is now available through the DBA navigator. There is a wizard available to walk through the scheduling of a full database backup and RMAN scripts can be generated to restore or recover a whole database, tablespaces, datafiles and archived logs. Built-in reporting is available to manage backup jobs, backup sets, image copies and RMAN settings.

Oracle Data Pump is also available from SQL Developer. This facilitates high speed movement of data and metadata from one database to another from the SQL Developer environment. With this user interface, you can import and export the full Database, Tablespaces, Schemas, or Tables. It is possible to import and export just the DDL, just the data or both.

Oracle Database 12c New Features

Setup a Global Database Service (GDS)

Database services are named representations of one or more database instances. Database services provide the following capabilities:

- Allow you to group database workloads
- Ensure that client requests are routed to the optimal instance that offers a service
- Transparently fail client connections over to surviving instances when a planned or unplanned instance outage occurs.

Oracle Global Data Services (GDS) implements the Oracle Database service model across a set of replicated databases known as a Global Data Services configuration. To database clients a GDS configuration appears as a virtual multi-instance database. Client access is provided through global services, which are functionally similar to local database services provided by single-instance or RAC databases. Global services span the instances of multiple databases, whereas local services span the instances of a single database. A GDS configuration and its global services are created and managed using the GDSCTL command-line interface. This tool is similar to the SRVCTL interface used to manage an Oracle RAC database and its services.

All administrative operations to Global Database Services should be performed using the appropriate GDSCTL commands. Many operations, such as adding a database to a Global Data Services pool, or enabling a global service, require making changes not only to the Global Data Services catalog, but also to databases in the Global Data Services configuration. The standard workflow for such commands is as follows:

- GDSCTL connects to the catalog database with credentials provided by the administrator and makes appropriate changes to the catalog.
- The catalog database notifies all global service managers in the Global Data Services configuration about the changes. The

notification is sent using an Oracle Net Services connection that each global service manager maintains with the catalog database.
- After receiving the notification one of the global service managers connects to the configuration databases that need to be configured and makes the appropriate changes.

There are several operations related to Global Services:

- **ADD SERVICE** -- The add service command creates a global service. When created, the global service is associated with a Global Data Services pool and its attributes stored in the Global Data Services catalog.
- **START SERVICE** -- This command is used to start a global service. A newly created global service never gets started automatically until the START SERVICE command is executed by the user. This gives the pool administrator control over the initial service startup.
- **STOP SERVICE** -- This command will shut down a global service running on databases in a Global Data Services pool. If the STOP SERVICE command is executed with the -database option, then the service is stopped on the specified databases; otherwise it is stopped on all databases in the pool.
- **DISABLE SERVICE** -- This command will disable a global service on a database or a set of databases. A disabled service cannot be started until it is re-enabled. This includes the service failover from another database; a database with the disabled service is never considered a failover target. A service can only be disabled if it is stopped.
- **ENABLE SERVICE** -- Allows a disabled service to be re-enabled. If the service management policy is AUTOMATIC and the database is eligible for running the service, it is started automatically after being enabled. A service with the MANUAL management policy must be started manually.
- **MODIFY SERVICE** -- This command allows is used to modify service properties (such as role, maximum lag, load balancing method, etc.). Service attributes also define on which databases the service should run. The command can be used to add a database to a service, remove it from a service, or move a service from one database to another.

- **REMOVE SERVICE** -- This command deletes a global service from the Global Data Services pool by removing it from the Global Data Services catalog and all databases where it was created. A service should be stopped before being deleted.

Define declarative policies for Oracle Data Redaction

Data Redaction provides runtime redaction of sensitive data being returned by SQL queries prior to being displayed by applications. This ensures that unauthorized users cannot view sensitive data. It provides consistent redaction of database columns across application modules accessing the same database information. Oracle Data Redaction allows you to redact column data by any of the following methods:

- **Full redaction** -- The entire contents of the column data is redacted. The redacted value returned to the querying application user depends on the data type of the column. Columns of the NUMBER data type are redacted with a zero (0), and character data types are redacted with a single space.
- **Partial redaction** -- Only a portion of the column data is redacted. For example, you can redact most of a credit card number with pound signs (#), except for the last 4 digits.
- **Regular expressions** -- Regular expressions can be used to look for patterns of data to redact. Designed for use with character data only, it is most applicable for data with varying character lengths.
- **Random redaction** -- The redacted data presented to the querying application user appears as randomly generated values each time it is displayed, depending on the data type of the column.
- **No redaction** -- The 'None' redaction type option enables you to test the internal operation of your redaction policies, with no effect on the results of queries against tables with policies defined on them.

Data Redaction policies define the way in which the data will be masked, including:

- What kind of redaction to perform (Full, Partial, Random, etc.)
- How the redaction should occur (e.g. for partial redaction, which portion of the data is redacted).
- When the redaction should take place (which users should see redacted vs. actual data).

EXECUTE privileges on the DBMS_REDACT PL/SQL package are required in order to create and manage an Oracle Data Redaction policy. The procedures in that package include the following:

- **DBMS_REDACT.ADD_POLICY** -- Adds a Data Redaction policy to a table or view
- **DBMS_REDACT.ALTER_POLICY** -- Modifies a Data Redaction policy
- **DBMS_REDACT.UPDATE_FULL_REDACTION_VALUES** -- Globally updates the full redaction value for a given data type. You must restart the database instance before the updated values can be used.
- **DBMS_REDACT.ENABLE_POLICY** -- Enables a Data Redaction policy
- **DBMS_REDACT.DISABLE_POLICY** -- Disables a Data Redaction policy
- **DBMS_REDACT.DROP_POLICY** -- Drops a Data Redaction policy

A full data redaction policy redacts the entire contents of a data column. By default, NUMBER data type columns are replaced with zero (0) and character data type columns are replaced with a single space. The UPDATE_FULL_REDACTION_VALUES procedure of the DBMS_REDACT package can be used to modify one or both of these defaults. The following example shows how to use full redaction for all the values in the TRGT.CUST_DATA table CC_NUM column. The expression parameter applies the policy to any user querying the table, except for users who have been granted the EXEMPT REDACTION POLICY system privilege.

```
BEGIN
  DBMS_REDACT.ADD_POLICY(
    object_schema => 'trgt',
    object_name   => 'cust_data',
    column_name   => 'cc_num',
    policy_name   => 'redact_cc_num',
    function_type => DBMS_REDACT.FULL,
    expression    => '1=1');
END;
```

When using partial data redaction, only a portion of the column data is redacted. A social security number might have all but the last four digits replaced with an asterisk for example (***-**-1234). It is possible to create policies for columns that use character, number, or date-time data types. For policies that redact character data types, there are a number of pre-defined character redaction shortcuts available. Some of the available shortcuts include:

- **DBMS_REDACT.REDACT_US_SSN_F5** -- Redacts the first 5 numbers of Social Security numbers when the column is a VARCHAR2 data type. For example, the number 987-65-4320 becomes XXX-XX-4320.
- **DBMS_REDACT.REDACT_US_SSN_L4** -- Redacts the last 4 numbers of Social Security numbers when the column is a VARCHAR2 data type. For example, the number 987-65-4320 becomes 987-65-XXXX.
- **DBMS_REDACT.REDACT_US_SSN_ENTIRE** -- Redacts the entire Social Security number when the column is a VARCHAR2 data type. For example, the number 987-65-4320 becomes XXX-XX-XXXX.
- **DBMS_REDACT.REDACT_ZIP_CODE** -- Redacts a 5-digit postal code when the column is a VARCHAR2 data type. For example, 95476 becomes XXXXX.
- **DBMS_REDACT.REDACT_DATE_MILLENNIUM** -- Redacts dates that are in the DD-MON-YY format to 01-JAN-00 (January 1, 2000).
- **DBMS_REDACT.REDACT_DATE_EPOCH** -- Redacts all dates to 01-JAN-70.

The following example shows how Social Security numbers in a VARCHAR2 data type column and can be redacted using the REDACT_US_SSN_L4 shortcut.

```
BEGIN
  DBMS_REDACT.ADD_POLICY(
    object_schema        => 'trgt',
    object_name          => 'cust_data',
    column_name          => 'ssn',
    policy_name          => 'redact_cust_ssns',
    function_type        => DBMS_REDACT.PARTIAL,
    function_parameters => DBMS_REDACT.REDACT_US_SSN_L4,
    expression           => '1=1',
    policy_description   => 'Partially redacts last 4 numbers in SS
numbers');
END;
```

The DBMS_REDACT.ADD_POLICY function_parameters parameter enables you to redact number data types. The value of this parameter determines how the redaction will take place. It accepts three values separated by commas:

- **Mask character** -- Specifies the character to display. This must be a number from 0 to 9.
- **Starting digit position** -- Specifies the starting digit position for the redaction.
- **Ending digit position** -- Specifies the ending digit position for the redaction.

The values must be entered in the order mask, start, end. The example below shows how to partially redact data from the SALARY field in the HR.EMPLOYEES table, for any application user who logs in. The below example will change the first four digits of each employee's salary to the number 9.

```
BEGIN
  DBMS_REDACT.ADD_POLICY(
     object_schema        => 'hr',
     object_name          => 'employees',
     column_name          => 'salary',
     policy_name          => 'redact_emp_sal',
     function_type        => DBMS_REDACT.PARTIAL,
     function_parameters  => '9,1,4',
     expression           => '1=1',
     policy_description   => 'Partially redacts salary');
END;
```

Apply best practices for running the ADDM Advisor

Automatic Database Diagnostic Monitor (ADDM) is a utility built into the Oracle database which automatically detects and reports performance problems. ADDM functionality is based on the snapshots taken by the Automatic Workload Repository (AWR). Data from the snapshots are analyzed and the results are displayed as ADDM findings on the Database Home page in Oracle Enterprise Manager Cloud Control. Cloud Control is the primary interface for diagnostic monitoring and whenever possible, you should run ADDM using it. If Cloud Control is unavailable, then it is also possible to run ADDM using the DBMS_ADDM package. In order to run the DBMS_ADDM APIs, the user must be granted the ADVISOR privilege.

ADDM findings allow administrators to quickly identify the performance problems affecting the database. Reviewing the findings of ADDM analysis should be one of the first steps in troubleshooting performance problems. Every ADDM finding will include one or more recommendations for reducing the impact of the performance problem. Regularly monitoring and implementing the recommendations from ADDM findings should be part of an administrator's routine maintenance process.

After each AWR snapshot is taken (hourly by default), an ADDM analysis is performed and the results saved in the database. If a potential performance problem is detected, ADDM then performs the following steps:

- Locates the root causes of the performance problem.
- Provides recommendations for correcting it.
- Quantifies the expected benefits.
- Identifies areas where no action is necessary.

ADDM analysis is performed from the top down. The utility identifies symptoms of performance issues and refines the analysis in an attempt to identify the root causes of the problem. ADDM uses the DB time statistic to identify performance problems. Database time is the cumulative time spent by the database in processing user requests. DB Time includes the wait time and CPU time of all non-idle user sessions. The ultimate goal is to minimize the DB time of the system for a given workload. This allows the database to service more user requests with a given set of resources.

Performance tuning is an iterative process. Any time one problem is resolved, another portion of the system may become a performance bottleneck. Resolving performance issues may take several cycles even with the benefit of the ADDM. When performance problems are identified, ADDM recommends potential solutions. If applicable, ADDM may recommend multiple solutions for a given problem. ADDM recommendations may include the following:

- **Hardware changes** -- Adding CPUs or changing the I/O subsystem configuration
- **Database configuration** -- Altering initialization parameter settings
- **Schema changes** – This could include hash partitioning a table or index, or using automatic segment space management (ASSM)
- **Application changes** – Examples might be using the cache option for sequences or using bind variables
- **Using other advisors** – This might include running SQL Tuning Advisor on high-load SQL statements or running the Segment Advisor on hot objects

ADDM is enabled in the database by default. It is controlled by the initialization parameters CONTROL_MANAGEMENT_PACK_ACCESS and STATISTICS_LEVEL. For ADDM to be enabled, CONTROL_MANAGEMENT_PACK_ACCESS should be set to DIAGNOSTIC+TUNING (default) or DIAGNOSTIC. Setting this parameter to NONE disables many Oracle Database features, including ADDM, and is strongly discouraged. The STATISTICS_LEVEL parameter should be set to TYPICAL (default) or ALL to enable ADDM. Setting this parameter to BASIC disables many Oracle Database features, including ADDM, and is strongly discouraged.

The analysis of I/O performance partially depends on the value of the DBIO_EXPECTED parameter. This parameter describes the expected performance of the I/O subsystem. The value is the average time in milliseconds that it takes to read a single database block. By default, Oracle uses a value of 10 milliseconds, which is appropriate for most hard drives. It is possible to choose a different value based on the characteristics of the hardware on the database server. If the appropriate value is determined to be different, it is possible to change the DBIO_EXPECTED value. The following statement will set DBIO_EXPECTED to 7000 microseconds when run as the SYS user:

```
EXECUTE DBMS_ADVISOR.SET_DEFAULT_TASK_PARAMETER('ADDM',
        'DBIO_EXPECTED', 7000);
```

The default settings for AWR are to generate snapshots of performance data once every hour, and retain the statistics in the workload repository for eight days. It is possible to change the default values for both the snapshot interval and the retention period. Oracle recommends that the retention period be set to at least one month. Longer periods may be advisable to span a full business cycle depending on the nature of the organization.

ADDM analysis results are represented as a set of findings. ADDM finding belongs to one of three classes:

- **Problem** -- Findings that describe the root cause of a database performance issue
- **Symptom** -- Findings that contain information that often leads to one or more problem findings
- **Information** -- Findings that are used to report areas of the system that do not have a performance impact

Every problem finding will be quantified with an estimate of the portion of DB time that resulted from it. If a problem has multiple causes, ADDM may report multiple findings for it. Recommendations are composed of actions and rationales. All actions of a given recommendation must be implemented in order to gain its estimated benefit. An ADDM action may present multiple solutions. If this is the case, then choose the easiest solution to implement.

Real-Time ADDM Analysis

Real-Time ADDM was originally introduced with Oracle Enterprise Manager Cloud Control 12c and is also available in Enterprise manager Express. Real-Time ADDM is designed to assist in the analysis and resolution of problems that cause unresponsive or hung databases. Traditionally performance problems that caused this would require the database to be restarted.

Real-Time ADDM analyzes the current performance of the database via a set of predefined criteria. If any problems are detected, Real-Time ADDM suggests methods for resolving any issues it identifies without restarting the database. Depending on the database state, Real-Time ADDM will use one of two connection modes to the database:

- **Normal connection** -- Real-Time ADDM performs a normal JDBC connection to the database. This mode is intended to perform extensive performance analysis of the database when some connectivity is available.

- **Diagnostic connection** -- This is a latch-less connection to the database that is intended for extreme hang situations when a normal JDBC connection is not possible.

Real-Time ADDM runs automatically every three seconds and uses in-memory data to locate performance spikes in the database. If a performance problem is detected, an analysis is triggered automatically. The scans are executed every three seconds by the manageability monitor process (MMON) to obtain performance statistics without lock or latch. MMON will analyze the statistics and trigger a Real-Time ADDM analysis if any of the following issues are detected.

- **High load** -- Average active sessions are greater than 3 times the number of CPU cores
- **I/O bound** -- I/O impact on active sessions based on single block read performance
- **CPU bound** -- Active sessions are greater than 10% of total load and CPU utilization is greater than 50%
- **Over-allocated memory** -- Memory allocations are over 95% of physical memory
- **Interconnect bound** -- Based on single block interconnect transfer time
- **Session limit** -- Session limit is close to 100%
- **Process limit** -- Process limit is close to 100%
- **Hung session** -- Hung sessions are greater than 10% of total sessions
- **Deadlock detected** -- Any deadlock is detected

The MMON slave process will then store the report that was created in the AWR. The report metadata can be accessed via the DBA_HIST_REPORTS view. Real-Time ADDM employs several controls to ensure that the automatic triggers do not consume too many system resources:

- **Duration between reports** -- If a Real-Time ADDM report was created in the past 5 minutes by the automatic trigger, then no new reports will be generated.
- **Oracle RAC control** -- Automatic triggers are local to the database instance. For Oracle RAC, only one database instance can create a Real-Time ADDM report at a given time because a lock is required and a query is performed by the MMON slave process before the report is actually generated.
- **Repeated triggers** -- An automatic trigger for any issue must have an impact of 100% or higher than the previous report with the same triggering issue within the past 45 minutes.
- **Newly identified issues** -- If a new issue is found that was not previously detected within the past 45 minutes, a new report is generated regardless of the new active sessions load.

Maximum Availability Architecture

Implement the various replication options available to the Oracle database

Oracle 12c contains five distinct options that provide replication capabilities: Oracle Streams, Oracle Advanced Replication, Oracle Data Guard, Oracle Advanced Data Guard, and Oracle GoldenGate. However, two of those, Oracle Streams and Oracle Advanced Replication, have been deprecated in Oracle Database Release 12c in favor of Oracle GoldenGate. While the options still exist in 12c and can be used by legacy applications -- the options are likely to be desupported and made unavailable in a future release. Questions about them are unlikely to be on the exam so this guide will concentrate on the other three.

Oracle GoldenGate

Oracle GoldenGate provides real-time data integration and replication in heterogeneous IT environments. Some of the features available with GoldenGate include:

- High availability solutions
- Real-time data integration
- Transactional change data capture
- Data replication
- Transformations
- Verification between operational and analytical enterprise systems

Oracle GoldenGate 12c allows organizations to capture, route, transform, and deliver transactional data between heterogeneous databases in real time with minimal overhead. Oracle GoldenGate captures and moves committed database transactions that meet ACID guidelines. It ensures the integrity of data as it is moved from the source database and applied to any number of target databases or messaging systems. The modular architecture or GoldenGate provides the flexibility to extract and replicate selected data records, transactional changes, and changes to DDL across a variety of topologies. Oracle GoldenGate consists of four distinct modules and components:

- **Oracle GoldenGate Capture** -- The Capture module grabs committed transactions resulting from insert, update, and delete operations executed against a database, and routes them for distribution.
- **Oracle GoldenGate Trail Files** -- GoldenGate's queuing mechanism generates files that contain the most recent changed data in a transportable, platform-independent format called the Oracle GoldenGate Universal Data Format.
- **Oracle GoldenGate Delivery** -- The Delivery module takes any changed transactional data that has been placed in a Trail File and immediately applies it to the target database.
- **Oracle GoldenGate Manager** -- The Manager module provides a command-line interface to perform a variety of administrative, housekeeping, and reporting activities.

Oracle Data Guard

Oracle Data Guard is included in the Oracle Database Enterprise Edition and is a major component of Oracle's High Availability architecture. Data Guard provides the software required to manage, monitor, and automate one or more standby databases. Standby databases help to protect Oracle data from failures, disasters, human error, and data corruptions. Simultaneously they provide high availability for mission critical applications.

A Data Guard configuration includes a production database (referred to as the primary database), and up to thirty directly connected replicas (referred to as standby databases). The primary and standby databases are connected via TCP/IP using Oracle Net Services. The databases do not need to be physically located in close proximity provided they can communicate with each other. A standby database is initially created from a backup of the primary database and then kept synchronized with the primary by Data Guard through the transmission and application of redo from the primary database redo.

Data Guard redo transport services can be either synchronous or asynchronous. Synchronous transport provides a guarantee of zero data loss if the primary database suddenly fails. However, synchronous redo transport requires the primary database to wait for confirmation from the standby that redo has been received and written to a standby redo log before commit success is signaled to the application. As the physical distance between the primary and standby database increases, so does the amount of time that the primary must wait to receive this acknowledgement. The increased wait time on commits will directly impact response time and throughput. The new Fast Sync option in Data Guard is designed to address this performance concern. Fast Sync allows the standby to acknowledge the primary database as soon as redo is received in memory. Not waiting for the disk I/O to occur can significantly reduce the performance impact of synchronous transport on the primary database.

Oracle Advanced Data Guard

Oracle Advanced Data Guard provides the same functionality as Data Guard plus a number of additional capabilities. These will be discussed in the next section.

Explain the architectural differences between Data Guard and Active Data Guard

Oracle Active Data Guard is also included as one of the options in the Oracle Database Enterprise Edition. Active Data Guard provides all of the functions of Data Guard plus advanced capabilities beyond it, including:

- **Real-Time Query** -- This function offloads read-only and read-mostly workloads that write to global temporary tables to an up-to-date standby database.
- **Automatic Block Repair** -- Physical corruptions of data are transparently repaired whether they occur in the primary or standby database. This prevents interruptions in service to users and eliminates the need for manual intervention by administrators.
- **Far Sync** -- This provides zero data loss protection even when the primary and standby databases are hundreds or thousands of miles apart. Far Sync also enables off-host network compression to conserve WAN bandwidth.
- **RMAN Block Change Tracking** -- Fast incremental backups are offloaded to an Active Data Guard Standby. This provides twenty times the performance of traditional incremental backups.
- **Active Data Guard Rolling Upgrade** -- This capability makes it easier to reduce planned downtime and minimizes the risk of introducing change to production systems.
- **Global Database Services** -- GDS provides intelligent load balancing and automated service management across replicated databases.
- **Application Continuity** -- When outages occur, this function works to make them transparent to users by handling in-flight transactions.

Active Data Guard is a licensed option of the Oracle Database Enterprise Edition. Making use of the Active Data Guard capabilities requires an Active Data Guard option license. The capabilities that are part of Data Guard do not require an option license to be used.

Implement the various Data Guard configurations available

An Oracle Data Guard configuration contains a single primary database and up to thirty destinations. All of the members in the configuration are connected by Oracle Net. They can be physically at the same location or may be dispersed geographically. So long as all members of the configuration can communicate with each other, there are no restrictions on where they are located.

Both primary and standby databases can be managed either through a SQL command-line interface or the via Oracle Data Guard broker interfaces. The broker contains both command-line interface (DGMGRL) and a graphical user interface that is built into Oracle Enterprise Manager Cloud Control. An Oracle Data Guard configuration will always contain one production database (known as the primary database). This is the database that that majority of applications access and functions in the primary role. It can be either a single-instance database or a Real Application Clusters database.

A standby database is a transactionally consistent copy of the primary database. Standby databases are created using a backup copy of the primary database. Oracle Data Guard automatically maintains each standby database by transmitting and applying redo information from the primary database to the standby. A standby database can also use either a single-instance or RAC configuration. There are four types of destinations available with Oracle Data Guard: Physical, Logical, Snapshot, and Far Sync.

Physical standby database

This configuration results in a physically identical copy of the primary database. All of the disk database structures will be identical to the primary database on a block-for-block basis. All of the schema objects in the database are the same as the primary. The datafiles in a physical standby database are kept synchronized with the primary database. Redo Apply accepts redo data received from the primary database and applies the changes in the redo to the physical standby database.

As of Oracle release 11.1, a physical standby database can be opened for read-only access and used to offload queries from a primary database. For databases that have an Oracle Active Data Guard license, Redo Apply can be active while the physical standby database is open. This capability allows queries to return results that are identical to what would be returned from the primary database. This is known as real-time query. A physical standby database can also be used to install eligible one-off patches, patch set updates (PSUs), and critical patch updates (CPUs), in rolling fashion.

A physical standby database provides the following benefits:

- **Disaster recovery and high availability** -- Switchover and failover capabilities allow for fast role reversals between primary and physical standby databases. This minimizes the downtime of the primary database for both planned and unplanned outages.
- **Data protection** -- A physical standby database can prevent data loss and facilitate rapid disaster recovery. All data types and all DDL and DML operations that are applicable to the primary database can be supported by a physical standby database. In addition, physical corruptions on the storage media of the primary database will not be propagated to a standby database. Logical corruptions or user errors that would otherwise cause data loss can be more easily resolved through the use of a standby database.
- **Reduction in primary database workload** -- Oracle Recovery Manager (RMAN) can use a physical standby database to off-load backups from a primary database. When using Active Data Guard, a physical standby database can also be queried while Redo Apply is active, allowing queries to be offloaded from the primary to a physical standby.
- **Performance** -- The Redo Apply technology used by a physical standby database is the most efficient mechanism for keeping a standby database updated with changes. The changes are made

using low-level recovery mechanisms which bypass all SQL level code layers.

Logical standby database

A logical standby database contains the same information as the production database. However, the physical organization and structure of the data may be different. As with a physical standby, a logical standby database is initially created as an identical copy of the primary database. A logical standby can later be altered to have a different structure. A logical standby database is kept synchronized with the primary database through SQL Apply, rather than Redo Apply. Rather than applying redo changes directly, SQL Apply transforms the data in the redo received from the primary database into SQL statements. The SQL statements are then executed on the standby database. Logical Standby databases must remain open so that updates via the SQL Apply operations can occur. While the logical standby database is opened in read/write mode, any target tables for the regenerated SQL are available only for read-only operations. The tables can be used for other tasks such as reporting, summations, and queries. There are some restrictions on a logical standby database regarding data types, types of tables, and types of DDL and DML operations that can be used. Review the Oracle Data Guard Concepts and Administration manual for more details.

A logical standby database provides the following benefits:

- **Minimizing downtime on software upgrades** -- A logical standby database greatly facilitates upgrading an Oracle Data Guard configuration in a rolling fashion. A logical standby can be upgraded to the new release and then switched over to become the active primary. The old primary is converted to a logical standby and the patchset is applied. During the patchset operation, access to the data is never interrupted.

- **Support for reporting and decision support requirements** -- Because logical standby databases do not have to be identical to the primary, additional structures can be created to optimize the reporting workload. A logical standby can have its tables physically reorganized into a different storage type with different partitioning. Alternately, additional indexes or materialized views can be created. However, a logical standby database does not allow for any transformation of data. It is not possible to replicate only a subset of columns or allow additional columns on user tables. Oracle GoldenGate software is the preferred solution for replication of that nature.

Snapshot Standby Database

A snapshot standby database is a fully updatable standby database. As with a physical or logical standby database, a snapshot standby database is created from a physical backup of the primary database and it receives and archives redo data from the primary database. However, a snapshot standby database does not apply that redo data as it is received. The received redo data is not applied until the snapshot standby is converted back into a physical standby database. Before applying the redo, the snapshot will discard any local updates made to the snapshot. A snapshot standby database is most applicable for situations that require a temporary, updatable snapshot of a physical standby database.

The nature of a snapshot standby database means that it will diverge from the primary database over time both because redo data from the primary database is not applied as well as divergence caused by local updates. The snapshot still provides data protection for the primary database, however, because a snapshot standby can be converted to a physical standby database at any time. At that time the local updates will be discarded and the redo data received from the primary applied. Disaster recovery from a snapshot standby will obviously take additional time over a physical standby due to the need to apply the redo data from the primary. It is also possible to create a snapshot standby, test, resynchronize with production, and then again create a snapshot standby. This cycle can be repeated as often as desired.

A snapshot standby database provides the following benefits:

- It provides an exact replica of a production database for development and testing purposes, while maintaining data protection at all times.
- It can be easily refreshed to contain current production data by converting to a physical standby and resynchronizing.

Far Sync Instance

An Oracle Data Guard far sync instance accepts redo from a primary database, but it does not itself act as a database. It is a remote destination that accepts redo from the primary database and then forwards it to other members of the Oracle Data Guard configuration. A far sync instance manages a control file, receives redo into standby redo logs (SRLs), and archives those SRLs to local archived redo logs. A far sync instance has no user data files, cannot be opened for access, cannot run redo apply, and cannot function in the primary role or be converted to any type of standby database. Far sync instances are part of the Oracle Active Data Guard Far Sync feature. A far sync instance provides the ability to failover to a terminal destination with zero data loss, and offloads some of the overhead from the primary database (like redo transport). Creating a far sync instance physically close to the primary will minimize the impact on commit response times due to reduced network latency between the primary and the far sync instance. At the same time, it allows for higher data protection.

Create an MAA architecture that leverages Active Data Guard and Oracle Golden Gate

It is possible to offload read-only and read-mostly workloads to Active Data Guard Standby replicas. This helps to reduce the workload on the primary server while simultaneously gaining additional benefits from the Standby database. Oracle GoldenGate replication also allows for the distribution of workloads over multiple databases, whether the databases are located in a single datacenter or multiple datacenters.

The new Global Data Services (GDS) available in Oracle 12c can provide dynamic, transparent, and automated load balancing and high availability across multiple datacenters. GDS extends the familiar notion of Database Services to span multiple database instances in near and far locations. Global Data Services provides failover, service management, and service load balancing to replicated database configurations that are very similar to that provided by RAC for a single database. Some of the benefits of Global Data Services (GDS) include:

- Higher Availability by supporting service failover across local and global databases.
- Better Scalability by providing load balancing across multiple databases.
- Better Manageability via centralized administration of global resources.

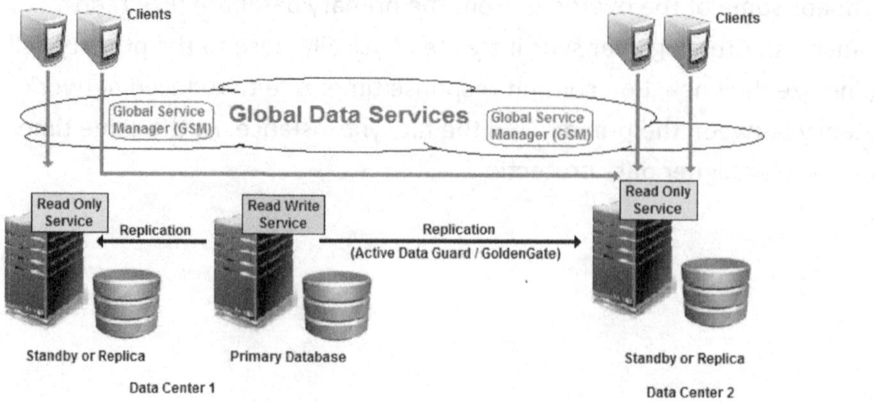

Global Data Services provides load balancing across replicated databases both within a single datacenter and across multiple datacenters. It will distribute the load across all of the databases available to it. In addition to the existing Oracle databases, GDS requires one or more Global Services Managers (GSMs), and a GDS Catalog Database. Each region will have its own GSM. The GSM is a server with specialized software that monitors database load and availability in order to appropriately direct the workload. To the application layer, the GSM looks like a listener.

The GDS Catalog is a database that hosts the metadata required for GDS to operate. The GSMs and the GDS Catalog act in concert with new GDS functionality in Oracle Database 12c. With GDS Data Guard still performs role transitions, but GDS is aware of them and directs load as appropriate.

Choose the appropriate high availability architecture based on various planned and unplanned scenarios

Planned scenarios that would normally involved downtime would include migration of part or all of a database. Various system and software maintenance operations can also require downtime. The various Oracle solutions that can perform each task include the following:

- **Migrate database to a different platform** -- Oracle Data Guard, Data Pump, Recovery Manager, or Oracle GoldenGate
- **Migrate database to a different character set** -- Oracle GoldenGate
- **Migrate to pluggable databases** -- Data Pump, Recovery Manager, or Oracle GoldenGate
- **Migrate storage** -- Oracle Automatic Storage Management or Oracle Data Guard
- **Migrate database from a single-instance system to an Oracle RAC cluster** -- Oracle Data Guard

- **Operating system and hardware upgrades** -- Oracle Real Application Clusters and Oracle Clusterware, Oracle RAC One Node, or Data Guard Standby-First Patch Apply
- **Oracle interim patches or diagnostic patches** -- Oracle Real Application Clusters and Oracle Clusterware, Oracle RAC One Node, or Online Patching
- **Oracle Database and Oracle Grid Infrastructure bundle patches, Patch Set Updates (PSU), Critical Patch Updates (CPU)** -- Data Guard Standby-First Patch Apply, Oracle Real Application Clusters and Oracle Clusterware, or Oracle RAC One Node
- **Oracle Database and Oracle Grid Infrastructure Patch Set and Major Upgrade** -- Oracle Data Guard
- **Upgrading Exadata storage** -- The Exadata PatchMgr utility
- **Application upgrades** -- Online Application Maintenance and Upgrades

Unplanned scenarios can include failures related to a site, instance/computer, storage, data corruption, human error, or file system data. For each of these, Oracle has one or more potential solutions that can be used to either maintain availability or reduce downtime. The solutions by failure type and their benefits follow:

Site failures

Oracle Data Guard and Oracle Application Failover (MAA recommended)

- Integrated client and application failover
- Fastest and simplest database replication
- Supports all data types
- Zero data loss by eliminating propagation delay
- Oracle Active Data Guard supports read-only services and DML on global temporary tables and sequences to off-load more work from the primary

Oracle GoldenGate

- Flexible logical replication solution (target is open read/write)
- Active-active high availability (with conflict resolution)
- Heterogeneous platform and heterogeneous database support

Recovery Manager and Oracle Secure Backup

- Fully managed database recovery and integration with Oracle Secure Backup
- Non-real-time recovery

Instance or computer failures

Oracle Real Application Clusters and Oracle Clusterware (MAA recommended)

- Integrated client and application failover
- Automatic recovery of failed nodes and instances
- Lowest application brownout with Oracle Real Application Clusters

Oracle RAC One Node

- Integrated client and application failover
- Online database relocation migrates connections and instances to another node
- Better database availability than traditional cold failover solutions

Oracle Data Guard

- Integrated client and application failover
- Fastest and simplest database replication
- Supports all data types

- Zero data loss by eliminating propagation delay
- Oracle Active Data Guard supports read-only services and DML on global temporary tables and sequences to off-load more work from the primary

Oracle GoldenGate

- Flexible logical replication solution (target is open read/write)
- Active-Active high availability (with conflict resolution)
- Heterogeneous platform and heterogeneous database support

Storage failures

Oracle Automatic Storage Management (MAA recommended)

- Mirroring and online automatic rebalancing places redundant copies of the data in separate failure groups.

Oracle Data Guard (MAA recommended)

- Integrated client and application failover
- Fastest and simplest database replication
- Supports all data types
- Zero data loss by eliminating propagation delay
- Oracle Active Data Guard supports read-only services and DML on global temporary tables and sequences to off-load more work from the primary

Recovery Manager with Fast Recovery Area and Oracle Secure Backup (MAA recommended)

- Fully managed database recovery and managed disk and tape backups

Oracle GoldenGate

- Flexible logical replication solution (target is open read/write)
- Active-active high availability (with conflict resolution)
- Heterogeneous platform and heterogeneous database support

Data corruption

Corruption Prevention, Detection, and Repair (MAA recommended)

- Database initialization settings such as DB_BLOCK_CHECKING, DB_BLOCK_CHECKSUM, and DB_LOST_WRITE_PROTECT offer different levels of block corruption prevention and detection at the database level

Oracle Data Guard (MAA recommended)

- In a Data Guard configuration having an Oracle Active Data Guard standby, physical block corruptions detected by Oracle at a primary database are automatically repaired using a good copy of the block retrieved from the standby, and vice versa. The repair is transparent to the user and application.
- The DB_LOST_WRITE_PROTECT initialization parameter provides lost write detection. If a lost write that occurred on the primary database is detected either by the physical standby database or during media recovery of the primary database, recovery is stopped to preserve the consistency of the database. However, failing over to the standby database using Data Guard will result in some data loss.
- If a lost write is detected on the standby database, you can restore the affected file and restart Redo Apply if the lost write is isolated and the hardware problem is corrected.

Data Recovery Advisor and Recovery Manager with Fast Recovery Area (MAA recommended)

- Data Recovery Advisor automatically detects data corruptions and recommends the best recovery plan.
- RMAN online block-media recovery time is very fast because RMAN can use flashback logs, backups, or the standby database to recover from physical block corruptions.

Oracle Exadata Database Machine and Oracle Automatic Storage Management (MAA recommended)

- If Oracle ASM detects a corruption and has a good mirror, Oracle ASM returns the good block and repairs the corruption during a subsequent write I/O.
- Exadata Cell provides implicit HARD enabled checks to prevent data corruptions caused by bad or misdirected storage I/O.

Oracle GoldenGate

- Flexible logical replication solution (target is open read/write). Logical replica can be used as a failover target if partner replica is corrupted.
- Active-active high availability (with conflict resolution)
- Heterogeneous platform and heterogeneous database support

Human errors

Oracle Security Features (MAA recommended)

- Restrict access to prevent human errors

Oracle Flashback Technology (MAA recommended)

- Fine-grained error investigation of incorrect results
- Fine-grained and database-wide rewind and recovery capabilities

Backup and Recovery

Explain general best practices and guidelines for backups on the Oracle database

The number one rule of any database and especially an enterprise database is to ensure that the information stored in it is never lost. The capabilities built into the Oracle database combined with a robust backup strategy should ensure that committed transactions will be recoverable under any failure scenario. The following practices can help to prevent an Oracle database from experiencing an unrecoverable data loss.

Logging Mode

Unless an Oracle database is one which is temporary or simply a testing platform, it will contain data that is worth recovering. If that is the case, the database should be configured in ARCHIVELOG mode. The initial archiving mode of Oracle is set in the CREATE DATABASE statement. The default is for the database to be in NOARCHIVELOG mode. Archiving the redo information generated by database creation is of no value, so the default is almost always used. After database creation, the mode should be changed to ARCHIVELOG for any database that might require data recovery.

The archiving mode of the database is set via the ALTER DATABASE statement with the ARCHIVELOG or NOARCHIVELOG clause. You must be connected to the database with SYSDBA privileges and the database must be mounted, but not open.

The steps to switch the database from NOARCHIVELOG to ARCHIVELOG are:

- **Shut down the database** -- The database must first be closed and any associated instances shut down.
- **Back up the database** -- The database should always be backed up before making major changes.
- **Set Parameters** -- You must edit the initialization parameter file to specify the archived redo log file destinations.
- **Start the instance in mount mode** -- The database cannot be open when changing the archive status.
- **Change the mode** -- Issue the ALTER DATABASE ARCHIVELOG command to place the database in archiving mode
- **Open the database** -- Issue an ALTER DATABASE OPEN.
- **Shut down the database** -- Issue a SHUTDOWN IMMEDIATE to shut down the instance and close the database.
- **Back up the database** -- You must back up all database files and the control file. Any previous backups cannot be used with the archived redo logs for recovery because they were not taken in ARCHIVELOG mode.

Archive log file destinations

When the database is in archivelog mode, at least one destination for archived log files must be specified. However, it is possible to specify two or more destinations to provide greater redundancy. The destinations can be either to a local file system, a remote file system, or to an Oracle Automatic Storage Management (Oracle ASM) disk group. If multiple destinations are specified, a copy of each filled redo log file will be written out to every destination simultaneously. If there is a failure at one of the destinations, Oracle can make use of a copy from one of the alternate destinations during recovery.

There are two methods by which you can set the archive log file destination.

LOG_ARCHIVE_DEST and LOG_ARCHIVE_DUPLEX_DEST -- For a single archive log destination, you can set only the LOG_ARCHIVE_DEST initialization parameters. To maintain a primary and secondary destination, you would specify the duplex location. These parameters can only be used for locations on the local host. Some examples are:

```
LOG_ARCHIVE_DEST = '/u01/arc'
LOG_ARCHIVE_DUPLEX_DEST = '/u02/arc'
```

LOG_ARCHIVE_DEST_n -- If you wish to archive to three or more locations, you must use the alternate LOG_ARCHIVE_DEST_n initialization parameters. The value of n can be any integer from 1 to 31. Archive destinations 1 to 10 are available for local or remote locations. Archive destinations 11 to 31 are available for remote locations only. Some examples are:

```
LOG_ARCHIVE_DEST_1 = 'LOCATION=/u01/arc'
LOG_ARCHIVE_DEST_2 = 'LOCATION=/u02/arc'
LOG_ARCHIVE_DEST_3 = 'LOCATION=/u03/arc'
```

The LOCATION keyword for LOG_ARCHIVE_DEST_n can be used to specify a file system location on the current host, an Oracle ASM disk group, or the Fast Recovery Area. Examples of each of these are:

```
LOG_ARCHIVE_DEST_n = 'LOCATION=/u01/arc'
LOG_ARCHIVE_DEST_n = 'LOCATION=+DGROUP1'
LOG_ARCHIVE_DEST_n = 'LOCATION=USE_DB_RECOVERY_FILE_DEST'
```

RMAN retention policy

RMAN retention policies are intended to insure that you have sufficient redundancy in the number of database backups to prevent a catastrophic data loss while keeping you from storing so many that you run out of disk space. The RMAN command CONFIGURE RETENTION POLICY is used to define an automatic backup retention policy. The backup retention policy provides RMAN with the information required to decide if a given backup of datafiles or control files is obsolete. Obsolete backups are no longer needed for recovery. These files can be viewed using the REPORT OBSOLETE command or removed using the DELETE OBSOLETE command

There are two different types of retention policy. It is only possible to use one of them -- they are mutually exclusive.

- **Recovery Window** -- This is a rolling window of time starting with the present and extending backward in time for a set length. A recovery window defines a point of recoverability, which will be the earliest time from which it is possible to recover following a media failure. If the defined recovery window is two weeks, then RMAN retains full backups and required incremental backups and archived logs that will allow the database to be recovered up to 14 days in the past. A recovery window policy is implemented as follows:

  ```
  CONFIGURE RETENTION POLICY TO RECOVERY WINDOW OF 14 DAYS;
  ```

- **Backup Redundancy** -- The redundancy retention policy specifies the number backups of each datafile to be retained. When there are more available than the number required, the oldest backups beyond the defined number are obsolete. The default retention policy is configured to REDUNDANCY 1. A backup redundancy of 3 is implemented as follows:

  ```
  CONFIGURE RETENTION POLICY TO REDUNDANCY 3;
  ```

Fast Recovery Area

The Fast Recovery Area is a location in which the database can store and manage files related to backup and recovery. The location is separate from the database area, where the current database files are located. The fast recovery area can contain control files, online redo logs, archived redo logs, flashback logs, and RMAN backups. Oracle's recommended practice is to enable archiving to the fast recovery area only and use disk mirroring for redundancy. Files in the recovery area are labeled as permanent or transient.

- **Permanent files** -- These are active files used by the database instance. Permanent files that can be in the recovery area include multiplexed copies of the current control file and online redo log files.
- **Transient files** -- These files are not accessed by the database instance and are needed only during recovery operations. Transient files include: archived redo log files, foreign archived redo log files, image copies of datafiles and control files, backup pieces, and flashback logs.

Transient files are generally deleted after they become obsolete or have been backed up to tape. Files placed in the fast recovery area are maintained by Oracle Database and the generated file names use the Oracle Managed Files (OMF) format. When files are no longer needed for recovery, they become eligible for deletion when space for new files is required.

The following initialization parameters are used to enable the Fast Recovery Area. Only the first two are required, and the database does not require a restart after they have been set.

- **DB_RECOVERY_FILE_DEST_SIZE** -- Specifies the maximum total bytes to be used by the Fast Recovery Area. The basic (minimum) recovery area size should be the sum of all the database files, plus sufficient size for incremental backups and all archive logs that have not been copied to tape. The required size varies widely depending on the backup strategy and whether flashback retention is enabled. This initialization parameter must be specified before DB_RECOVERY_FILE_DEST is enabled.
- **DB_RECOVERY_FILE_DEST** -- Location of the Fast Recovery Area. This can be a directory, file system, or Automatic Storage Management (Oracle ASM) disk group. It cannot be a raw file system.
- **DB_FLASHBACK_RETENTION_TARGET** -- Specifies the upper limit (in minutes) on how far back in time the database may be flashed back. This parameter is required only for Flashback Database.

RMAN Recovery Catalog

The RMAN recovery catalog is a database schema in an Oracle database that is used to store metadata about one or more Oracle databases. The data from this schema is used by RMAN when performing recovery operations. While the catalog can be stored in a database used for other purposes, it is generally stored in a dedicated database. The catalog stores information about RMAN operations for all of the target databases that have been registered in it. Any time that RMAN is connected to a recovery catalog, all metadata will be pulled exclusively from the catalog instead of the control file. By centralizing the metadata for all your target databases, the recovery catalog makes reporting and administration easier. A recovery catalog includes:

- Datafile and archived redo log backup sets and backup pieces
- Datafile copies
- Archived redo logs and their copies
- Database structure (tablespaces and datafiles)
- Stored scripts, which are named user-created sequences of RMAN commands
- Persistent RMAN configuration settings

A Recovery Catalog is required in the following situations:

- **Loss of control files** -- If the current control file and all backups are lost for a given database, a recovery catalog is required. Recovery catalogs contain the same metadata as the RMAN repository stored in the control file of each target database.
- **Recovery from very old backup** -- The control file contains a more limited amount of history than a recovery catalog. If you need to perform a recovery from a backup that goes back further in time than is stored in the control file, then a recovery catalog is required.
- **RMAN Scripts** -- RMAN scripts can be stored in a recovery catalog. The scripts are then available to every RMAN client that can connect to the target database and recovery catalog. By contrast,

command files are only available if the RMAN client has access to the file system on which they are stored.

- **Data Guard** -- If you want to use RMAN in a Data Guard environment, a recovery catalog is required. The recovery catalog stores RMAN metadata for all primary and standby databases.

Implement recovery procedures for various failure scenarios

There are dozens of potential failure scenarios that can require an administrator to perform recovery on the database. A handful of the more common failure scenarios follow.

Recover from a lost TEMP file

If one of more files belonging to the temporary tablespace is lost, any SQL statements that require space in the temporary tablespace will generate an error. If the database is up and you would like to recreate the file immediately, you can do so by creating a new datafile and dropping the old one as follows:

```
SQL> ALTER TABLESPACE temp ADD TEMPFILE
'/u01/app/oracle/oradata/orcl/temp02.dbf' SIZE 50M;
SQL> ALTER TABLESPACE temp DROP TEMPFILE
'/u01/app/oracle/oradata/orcl/temp01.dbf';
```

If the loss or damage to the datafile occurred while the database is down, simply starting the instance will automatically recreate the datafile. If Oracle detects a missing datafile on startup, it will issue the commands to recreate it. You will see a message in the alert log such are:

```
Re-creating tempfile /u01/app/oracle/oradata/orcl/temp01.dbf
```

If the file damage occurred while the database is started, but you would prefer to have the recovery done automatically (and assuming that restarting the database is an option), then shutting down and restarting the instance will recreate the file.

Recover from a lost redo log group

If all members of an online redo log group are damaged, the recovery process depends on the type of online redo log group affected and the whether or not the database is in archivelog mode. If the damaged online redo log group is current and active, then it is needed for crash recovery; otherwise, it is not. You can determine the status of the group associated with the damage files from V$LOGFILE:

```
SELECT group#, status, member
FROM   v$logfile;

GROUP#     STATUS        MEMBER
-------    -----------   ----------------------
0001                       /oracle/dbs/log1a.f
0001                       /oracle/dbs/log1b.f
0002       INVALID         /oracle/dbs/log2a.f
0002       INVALID         /oracle/dbs/log2b.f
0003                       /oracle/dbs/log3a.f
0003                       /oracle/dbs/log3b.f
```

You can determine which groups are active from the V$LOG view:

```
SELECT group#, status, archived
FROM   v$log;

GROUP#  STATUS     ARCHIVED
------  ---------  -----------
 0001   INACTIVE   YES
 0002   ACTIVE     NO
 0003   CURRENT    NO
```

If all members of an inactive online redo log group are damaged, then the procedure depends on whether it is possible to repair the media problem that damaged the group. If the failure is transient, then fix the problem. The log writer will reuse the redo log group when required. For permanent failures, the damaged redo log group will halt normal database operation when the database tries to use it. The damaged group must be reinitialized manually by issuing the ALTER DATABASE CLEAR LOGFILE statement.

If all members of an active (but not current) log group are damaged and the database is still running, issue the ALTER SYSTEM CHECKPOINT statement. If the checkpoint is successful, then the redo log group will become inactive. At this point you can follow the steps for an inactive online redo log group. If the checkpoint is unsuccessful, or the database has halted, then depending on the archiving mode you must follow the recovery procedures corresponding to the current log group.

The current log group is the one LGWR is currently writing to. If a LGWR I/O operation fails, then LGWR terminates and the instance is terminated. In this case, you must restore a backup, perform incomplete recovery, and open the database with the RESETLOGS option.

Recovering from the Loss of Active Logs in NOARCHIVELOG Mode

- If the media failure is temporary, then correct the problem so that the database can reuse the group when required.
- Restore the database from a consistent, whole database backup (data files and control files).
- Mount the database:
- To allow the database to reset the online redo logs, you must first mimic incomplete recovery:
```
RECOVER DATABASE UNTIL CANCEL
CANCEL
```
- Open the database using the RESETLOGS option:
```
ALTER DATABASE OPEN RESETLOGS;
```

- Shut down the database consistently.
```
SHUTDOWN IMMEDIATE
```

- Make a full database backup.

Recovering from Loss of Active Logs in ARCHIVELOG Mode

- Begin incomplete media recovery, recovering up through the log before the damaged log.
- Ensure that the current name of the lost redo log can be used for a newly created file. If not, then rename the members of the damaged online redo log group to a new location.
- Open the database using the RESETLOGS option:
```
ALTER DATABASE OPEN RESETLOGS;
```

Perform Full database recovery with RMAN

- Start RMAN and connect to a target database.
```
% rman
RMAN> CONNECT TARGET /
```

- If the database is not mounted, then mount but do not open the database.
```
STARTUP MOUNT;
```

- Use the SHOW command to see which channels are preconfigured.
```
SHOW ALL;
```

- If the necessary devices and channels are already configured, then no action is necessary. Otherwise, you can use the CONFIGURE command to configure automatic channels, or include ALLOCATE CHANNEL commands within a RUN block.
- Restore and recover the database.
```
RMAN> RESTORE DATABASE;
Starting restore at 20-FEB-14
.
.
.
Finished restore at 20-FEB-14

RMAN> RECOVER DATABASE;
```

```
Starting recover at 20-FEB-14
.
.
.
media recovery complete, elapsed time: 00:00:21
Finished recover at 20-FEB-14
```

- Examine the output to see if media recovery was successful. If so, open the database.
  ```
  ALTER DATABASE OPEN;
  ```

Use the Data Recovery Advisor for backup and recovery solutions

Oracle's Data Recovery Advisor is a data corruption repair function integrated with Support Workbench, database health checks and RMAN. It can display data corruption problems, assess their extent and impact, recommend repair options, and automate the repair process. In the context of Data Recovery Advisor, a health check is a diagnostic procedure run by the Health Monitor to assess the state of the database or its components. Health checks are invoked reactively when an error occurs and can also be invoked manually.

Failures

A failure is a persistent data corruption detected by a health check. They are usually detected reactively when a database operation encounters corrupted data and generates an error. This will automatically invoke a health check in the database. The check will search the database for failures related to the error and record any findings in the Automatic Diagnostic Repository. Data Recovery Advisor can generate repair advice and repair failures only after failures have been detected by the database and stored in the ADR. Data Recovery Advisor can report on and repair failures such as inaccessible files, physical and logical block corruptions, and I/O failures. All failures are assigned a priority: CRITICAL, HIGH, or LOW, and a status of OPEN or CLOSED.

- **CRITICAL** priority failures require immediate attention because they make the whole database unavailable. Typically, critical failures bring down the instance and are diagnosed during the subsequent startup.
- **HIGH** priority failures make a database partially unavailable or unrecoverable, and usually have to be repaired in a reasonably short time.
- **LOW** priority indicates that failures can be ignored until more important failures are fixed.

DRA Repairs

Data Recovery Advisor allows you to view repair options. Repairs might involve the use of block media recovery, datafile media recovery, or Oracle Flashback Database. In general, Data Recovery Advisor presents both automated and manual repair options. If appropriate, you can choose an automated repair option in order to perform a repair. In an automated repair, Data Recovery Advisor performs the repair, verifies the repair success, and closes the relevant failures.

The recommended workflow for repairing data failures from RMAN is to run the following commands in sequence during an RMAN session: LIST FAILURE to display failures, ADVISE FAILURE to display repair options, and REPAIR FAILURE to fix the failures.

LIST FAILURE

The LIST FAILURE command displays failures against which you can run the ADVISE FAILURE and REPAIR FAILURE commands.

```
RMAN> LIST FAILURE;
List of Database Failures
=========================
Failure ID Priority Status  Time Detected Summary
---------- -------- ------- ------------- ------------------------
274        HIGH     OPEN    12-FEB-14     One or more non-system
                                          datafiles are missing
329        HIGH     OPEN    12-FEB-14     Datafile 1:

'/u01/oradata/prod/system01.dbf'
                                          contains one or more
corrupt blocks
```

ADVISE FAILURE

Use the ADVISE FAILURE command to display repair options for the specified failures. This command prints a summary of the failures identified by the Data Recovery Advisor and implicitly closes all open failures that are already fixed. The ADVISE FAILURE command indicates the repair strategy that Data Recovery Advisor considers optimal for a given set of failures. Data Recovery Advisor verifies repair feasibility before proposing a repair strategy. For example, it will check that all backups and archived redo log files needed for media recovery are available. It can generate both manual and automated repair options.

The ADVISE command maps a set of failures to the set of repair steps that Data Recovery Advisor considers to be optimal. When possible, Data Recovery Advisor consolidates multiple repair steps into a single repair. For example, if the database has corrupted datafile, missing control file, and lost current redo log group, then Data Recovery Advisor would recommend a single, consolidated repair plan to restore the database and perform point-in-time recovery.

```
RMAN> ADVISE FAILURE;
List of Database Failures
=========================
Failure ID Priority Status  Time Detected Summary
---------- -------- ------- ------------- ----------------------
274        HIGH     OPEN    12-FEB-14     One or more non-system
                                          datafiles are missing
329        HIGH     OPEN    12-FEB-14     Datafile 1:
'/u01/oradata/prod/system01.dbf'
                                          contains one or more
corrupt blocks

analyzing automatic repair options; this may take some time
using channel ORA_DISK_1
analyzing automatic repair options complete

Mandatory Manual Actions
========================
no manual actions available

Optional Manual Actions
=======================
1. If file /u01/oradata/prod/data01.dbf was unintentionally renamed
or moved, restore it

Automated Repair Options
========================
Option Repair Description
---------------------------------------------
Restore and recover datafile 31; Perform block
    media recovery of block 43481 in file 1

Strategy: The repair includes complete media recovery with no data
loss
Repair script:
/u01/oracle/log/diag/rdbms/prod/prod/hm/reco_740113269.hm
```

CHANGE FAILURE

The CHANGE FAILURE command allows you to change the failure priority from HIGH to LOW or the reverse, or to close it. You cannot change to or from CRITICAL priority.

```
RMAN> CHANGE FAILURE 3 PRIORITY LOW;
```

REPAIR FAILURE

The REPAIR FAILURE command is used to repair database failures identified by the Data Recovery Advisor. The target database instance must be started. It must be a single-instance database and cannot be a physical standby database. It is important that at most one RMAN session is running the REPAIR FAILURE command. The only exception is REPAIR FAILURE ... PREVIEW, which is permitted in concurrent RMAN sessions. To perform an automated repair, the Data Recovery Advisor may require specific backups and archived redo logs. If the files are not available, then the recovery will not be possible. Data Recovery Advisor consolidates repairs whenever possible so that a single repair can fix multiple failures. If one has not yet been issued in the current RMAN session, REPAIR FAILURE performs an implicit ADVISE FAILURE. RMAN always verifies that failures are still relevant and automatically closes failures that have already been repaired. After executing a repair, RMAN reevaluates all open failures on the chance that some of them may also have been fixed.

Monitoring

Use Oracle Enterprise Manager to view database storage structures

Oracle Enterprise Manager Express (EM Express) has the ability to perform a number of basic administrative capabilities. From the web interface, you can view, create, and alter the various storage structures of the database. When you first log into EM Express, you will be presented with a page similar to the below:

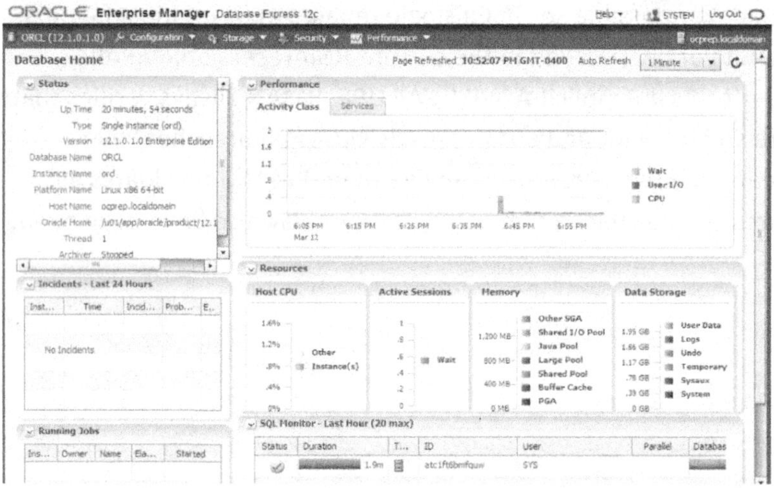

At the top of the screen, the second option from the left is 'Storage'. Clicking this will open a drop-down menu of the various storage structure types in an Oracle database. Selecting an option will open one of the following screens.

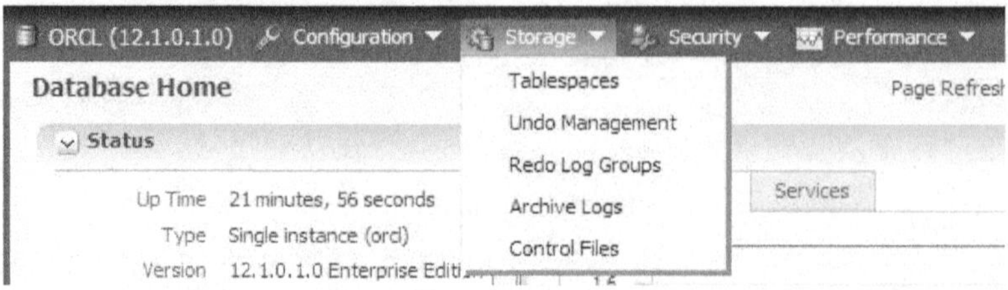

Tablespaces

This screen allows you to perform standard administrative options related to tablespaces, including creating, dropping, adding datafiles, changing the status (i.e. to read-only), and more.

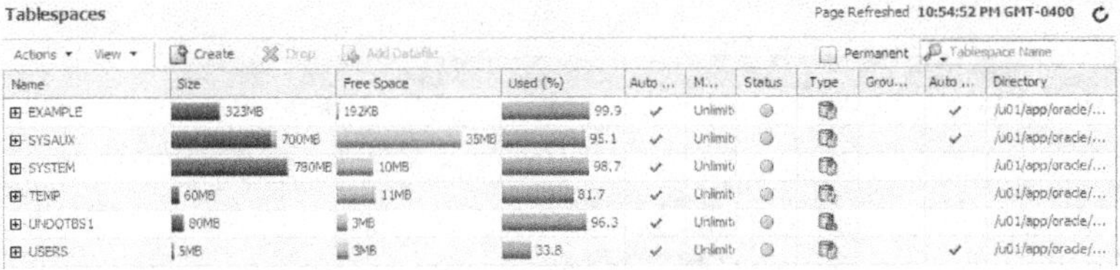

Undo Management

This primary purpose of this screen is to display statistics about the undo tablespace. There is seldom a need for a second undo tablespace and the one tablespace requires little management. This screen is primarily useful in verifying that your undo tablespace is sized correctly for the activity in your database.

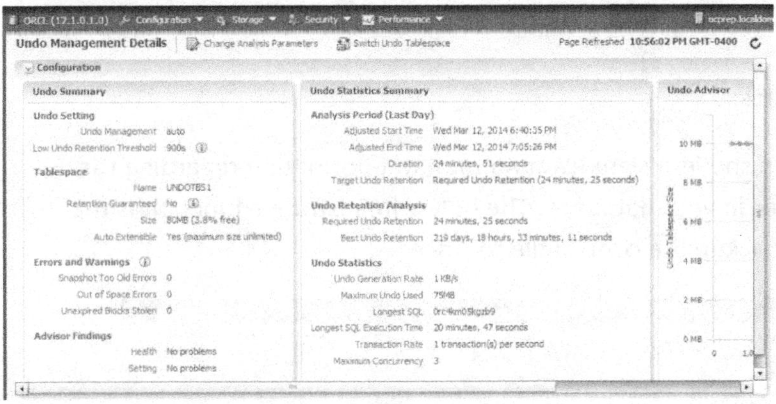

Redo Log Groups

As with the tablespaces screen, this page allows you to perform multiple administrative functions on the redo log groups: creating, dropping, adding members, and so on. You can easily see which log group is current, if a group has been archived, and more.

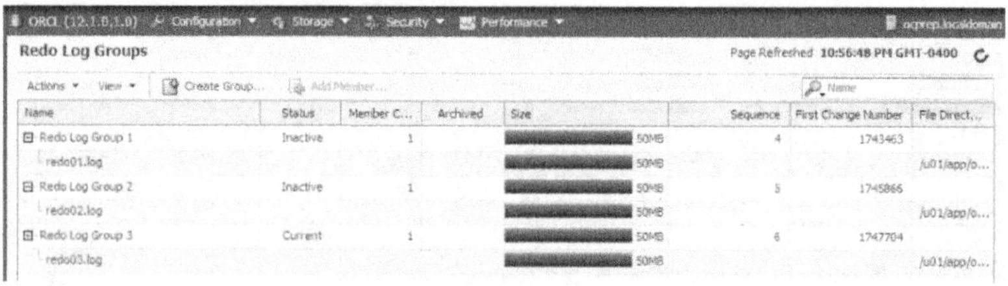

Archive Logs

This screen allows you to view information about archive logs.

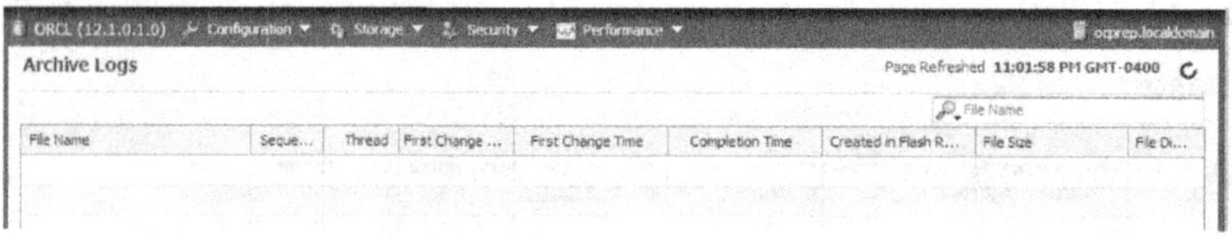

Control Files:

This screen shows a significant amount of information regarding the control files in your database. The only administrative function is the ability to backup the control file to trace.

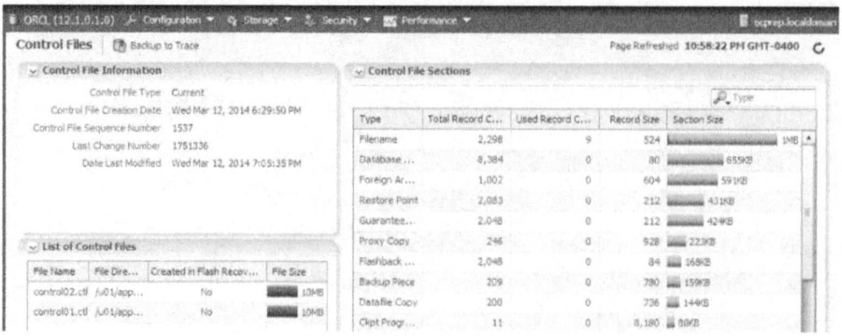

Apply different strategies for interacting with the database using SQL Developer

The SQL Developer interface has hundreds of different ways to interact with the database. Covering even a small fraction of the total in a single chapter is simply not feasible. The exam designers are most likely referring to the differences in interacting with the database through traditional SQL commands vs. doing so through the graphical interface. SQL Developer supports the vast majority of the commands that Oracle professionals who have used SQL*Plus in the past are familiar with. For example, it is possible to describe the structure of the HR.EMPLOYEES table with the use of the DESC command in a SQL Worksheet window as shown below.

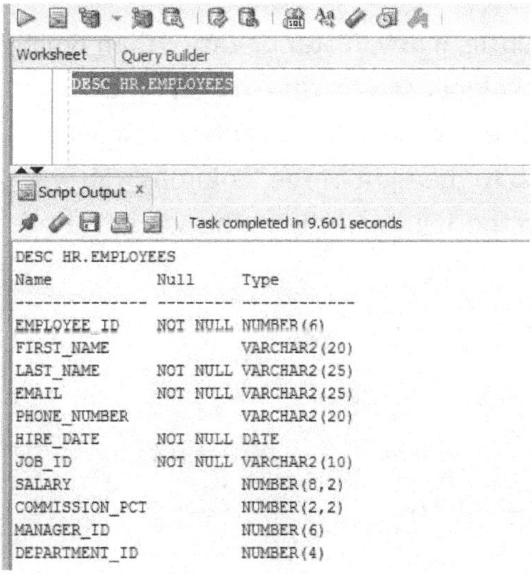

However, SQL Developer also supports much of the same functionality through the GUI interface. The GUI tools often make administration of database objects easier than the equivalent text commands. The example below shows how it is possible to display the structure of a table through the GUI interface. The steps to show the HR.EMPLOYEES table structure through the graphical interface and the result in SQL Developer are shown below:

- Click the 'Other Users' folder to open it.
- Click the 'HR' user to open it.
- Click the 'EMPLOYEES' table.

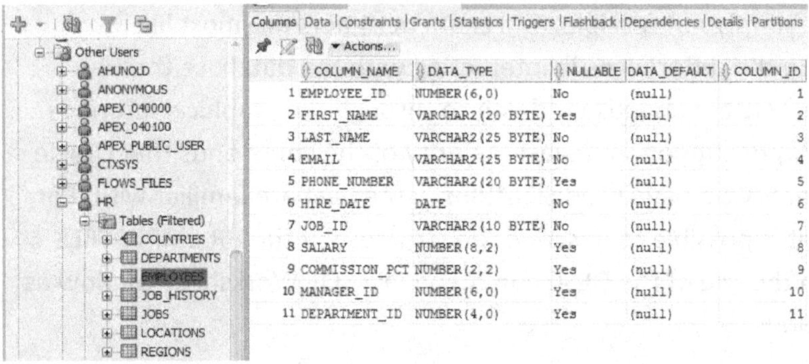

	COLUMN_NAME	DATA_TYPE	NULLABLE	DATA_DEFAULT	COLUMN_ID
1	EMPLOYEE_ID	NUMBER(6,0)	No	(null)	1
2	FIRST_NAME	VARCHAR2(20 BYTE)	Yes	(null)	2
3	LAST_NAME	VARCHAR2(25 BYTE)	No	(null)	3
4	EMAIL	VARCHAR2(25 BYTE)	No	(null)	4
5	PHONE_NUMBER	VARCHAR2(20 BYTE)	Yes	(null)	5
6	HIRE_DATE	DATE	No	(null)	6
7	JOB_ID	VARCHAR2(10 BYTE)	No	(null)	7
8	SALARY	NUMBER(8,2)	Yes	(null)	8
9	COMMISSION_PCT	NUMBER(2,2)	Yes	(null)	9
10	MANAGER_ID	NUMBER(6,0)	Yes	(null)	10
11	DEPARTMENT_ID	NUMBER(4,0)	Yes	(null)	11

While the three-click process was little, if any, faster or easier than typing 'DESC HR.EMPLOYEES', the SQL developer screen that displays the structure of the table also has a suite of other options only a click away. For example, clicking the 'Data' tab to the right of the 'Columns' tab will display the data of the table. From the SQL Worksheet, this would be equivalent to:

```
SELECT * FROM HR.EMPLOYEES;
```

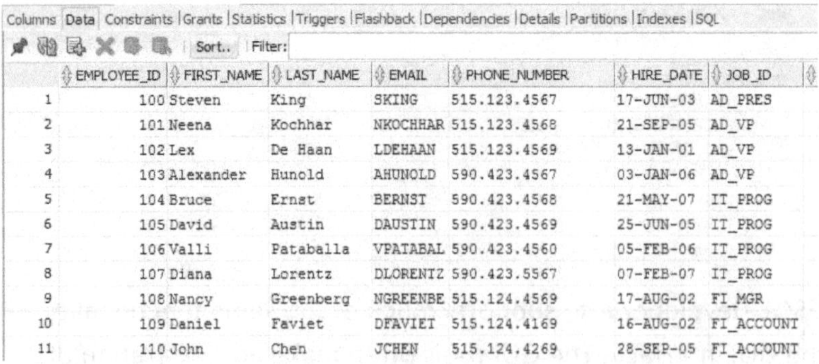

	EMPLOYEE_ID	FIRST_NAME	LAST_NAME	EMAIL	PHONE_NUMBER	HIRE_DATE	JOB_ID
1	100	Steven	King	SKING	515.123.4567	17-JUN-03	AD_PRES
2	101	Neena	Kochhar	NKOCHHAR	515.123.4568	21-SEP-05	AD_VP
3	102	Lex	De Haan	LDEHAAN	515.123.4569	13-JAN-01	AD_VP
4	103	Alexander	Hunold	AHUNOLD	590.423.4567	03-JAN-06	AD_VP
5	104	Bruce	Ernst	BERNST	590.423.4568	21-MAY-07	IT_PROG
6	105	David	Austin	DAUSTIN	590.423.4569	25-JUN-05	IT_PROG
7	106	Valli	Pataballa	VPATABAL	590.423.4560	05-FEB-06	IT_PROG
8	107	Diana	Lorentz	DLORENTZ	590.423.5567	07-FEB-07	IT_PROG
9	108	Nancy	Greenberg	NGREENBE	515.124.4569	17-AUG-02	FI_MGR
10	109	Daniel	Faviet	DFAVIET	515.124.4169	16-AUG-02	FI_ACCOUNT
11	110	John	Chen	JCHEN	515.124.4269	28-SEP-05	FI_ACCOUNT

The data displayed can be filtered by adding a condition to the 'Filters' box. Adding LAST_NAME='King' to that box provides the same results as the SQL Query:

```
SELECT *
FROM   HR.EMPLOYEES
WHERE  LAST_NAME='King';
```

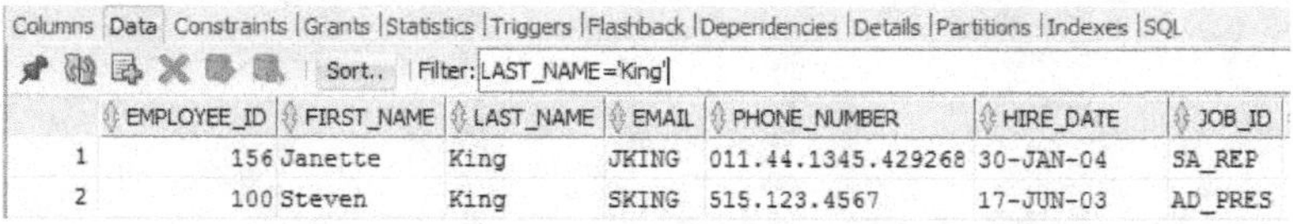
Columns | Data | Constraints | Grants | Statistics | Triggers | Flashback | Dependencies | Details | Partitions | Indexes | SQL

Sort.. | Filter: LAST_NAME='King'

	EMPLOYEE_ID	FIRST_NAME	LAST_NAME	EMAIL	PHONE_NUMBER	HIRE_DATE	JOB_ID
1	156	Janette	King	JKING	011.44.1345.429268	30-JAN-04	SA_REP
2	100	Steven	King	SKING	515.123.4567	17-JUN-03	AD_PRES

Clicking on the 'Constraints' tab will display all of the constraints associated with HR.EMPLOYEES. This would be roughly equivalent to the SQL command:

```
SELECT *
FROM   ALL_CONSTRAINTS
WHERE  TABLE_NAME = 'EMPLOYEES'
AND    OWNER = 'HR';
```

The result is not exactly equivalent, because SQL Developer does not display the table name and owner (since those are known), and it displays constraint names (Foreign_Key, Check, Unique) instead of the abbreviations in the ALL_CONSTRAINTS table (R, C, and U respectively).

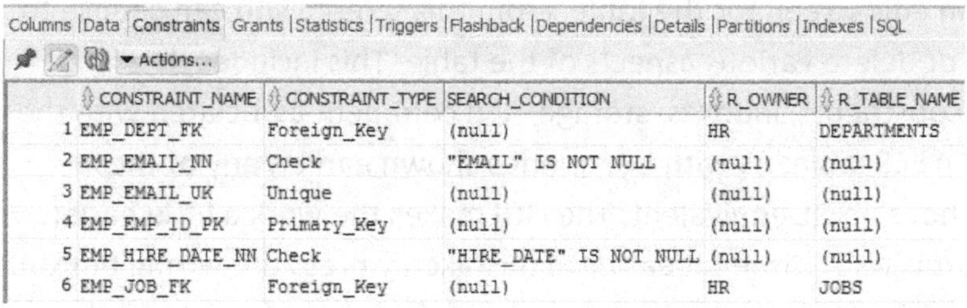
Columns | Data | Constraints | Grants | Statistics | Triggers | Flashback | Dependencies | Details | Partitions | Indexes | SQL

Actions...

	CONSTRAINT_NAME	CONSTRAINT_TYPE	SEARCH_CONDITION	R_OWNER	R_TABLE_NAME
1	EMP_DEPT_FK	Foreign_Key	(null)	HR	DEPARTMENTS
2	EMP_EMAIL_NN	Check	"EMAIL" IS NOT NULL	(null)	(null)
3	EMP_EMAIL_UK	Unique	(null)	(null)	(null)
4	EMP_EMP_ID_PK	Primary_Key	(null)	(null)	(null)
5	EMP_HIRE_DATE_NN	Check	"HIRE_DATE" IS NOT NULL	(null)	(null)
6	EMP_JOB_FK	Foreign_Key	(null)	HR	JOBS

The next tab displays all grants made to the HR.EMPLOYEES table, equivalent to the following query:

```
SELECT *
FROM   ALL_TAB_PRIVS
WHERE  TABLE_NAME = 'EMPLOYEES';
```

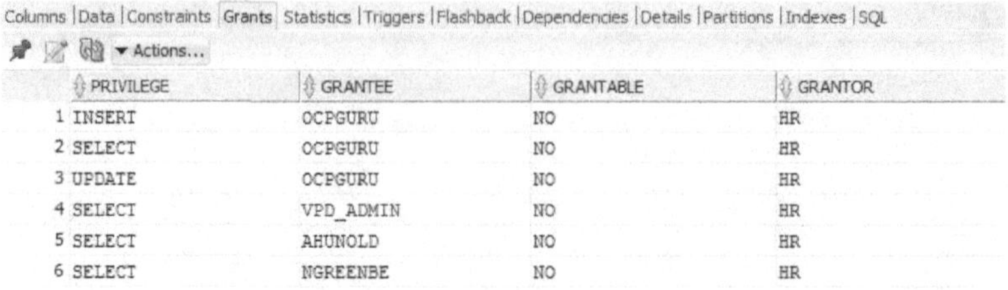

	PRIVILEGE	GRANTEE	GRANTABLE	GRANTOR
1	INSERT	OCPGURU	NO	HR
2	SELECT	OCPGURU	NO	HR
3	UPDATE	OCPGURU	NO	HR
4	SELECT	VPD_ADMIN	NO	HR
5	SELECT	AHUNOLD	NO	HR
6	SELECT	NGREENBE	NO	HR

The remaining tabs show additional information about the table statistics, triggers, and so forth. Each displays information that could be reproduced by an equivalent SQL command. The GUI interface makes this information considerably more accessible – especially if you cannot recall the names of various data dictionary views off the top of your head.

What makes SQL Developer a very useful tool is the fact that it is completely tied in to the Oracle data dictionary. Each of the 'folders' shown in the Connections window is linked to a class of object stored in the data dictionary. Opening the folder displays all of that type of object. You can then select an individual object of that class and find out all the information about it that is stored in the data dictionary. Beyond that, you can use SQL Developer to edit the object.

Going back to the HR.EMPLOYEES table, clicking on the 'Pencil' icon will open up an edit screen for the table. From this screen, you can choose to add, edit, or delete various aspects of the table. This includes the columns, constraints, indexes, storage, and comment associated with the HR.EMPLOYEES table. As with the queries shown earlier, any of these functions have a SQL equivalent. The GUI makes the work a little easier. That said, it is also a little bit easier to mistakenly press the wrong button, delete the wrong column, or in any number of ways cause some real damage to a database object. DDL is dangerous whether it is issued from the command line or from a GUI.

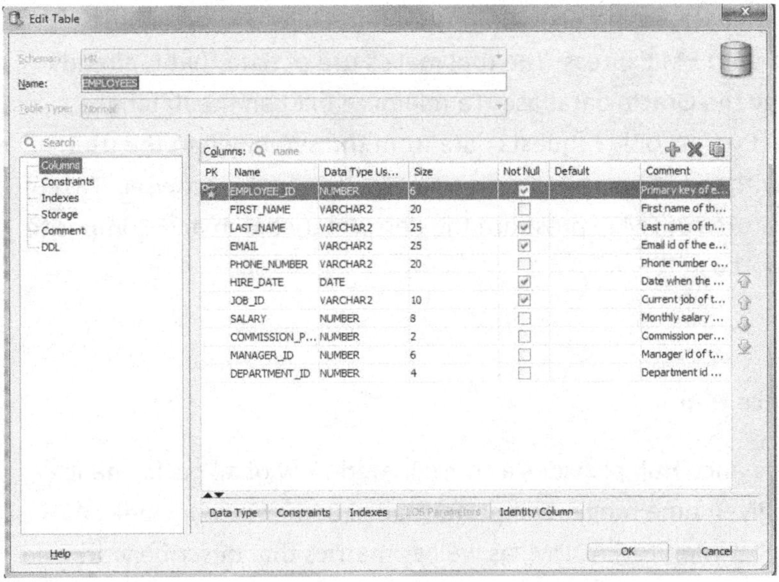

Describe the EM Cloud Control and EM Express architecture as it relates to the database

EM Express

This is a web-based tool for managing Oracle Database 12c that is built into the database server. EM Express provides the ability to perform basic administrative tasks such as storage and user management as well as the ability to diagnose performance issues and tune the database. EM Express is a lightweight tool designed to incur minimal overhead on the database server. EM Express uses no middle-tier components at all -- only internal infrastructure components of Oracle such as XDB and SQL*Net. For this reason, the database must be open in order to use EM Express, and the utility can perform no actions outside the database. Unlike Enterprise Manager Cloud Control, EM Express can neither start nor shut down an Oracle database.

There are no background tasks or information-collecting processes associated with EM Express. The tool makes use of data that is already collected by the Oracle database. To minimize load on the database server, EM Express only requests data from the server when the user interacts with the UI and all UI processing is done in the browser. Two of the key features of EM Express are the Performance Hub and Composite Active Reports.

Performance Hub

The Performance Hub provides a consolidated view of all performance data for a given time range. The performance data shown includes ASH Analytics, SQL Monitor, ADDM, as well as metrics that describe workload characteristics and database resource usage.

The Performance Hub can be used to view both historical and real-time data. A time range can be selected using a time picker at the top of the page, and the detail tabs will display the available performance data for the selected time range. The time picker displays average active sessions over time. When there are peaks in the time picker, the selected time range can be moved to the period of interest to gain more information.

When functioning in real-time mode, performance data is retrieved from in-memory views. The time picker shows data for the past hour and the user can select any time range from within this period. The default selection is the past 5 minutes. When functioning in historical mode, data is retrieved from the Automatic Workload Repository (AWR). The user can select any time period, provided there is sufficient data in AWR. The Performance Hub can also be saved as a Composite Active Report.

The Performance Hub organizes performance data by dividing it into different tabs that address a specific aspect of database performance. The tabs available in the Performance Hub are:

- **Summary** -- In real-time mode, this tab shows metrics data that gives an overview of system performance in terms of Host Resource Consumption (CPU, I/O and Memory), and Average Active Sessions. In historical mode, the tab displays system performance in terms of resource consumption, average active sessions, and load profile information.
- **Activity** -- Displays ASH Analytics in both real-time and historical mode.
- **Workload** -- Displays metric information about the workload profile, such as call rates, logon rate and the number of sessions. In addition, the tab also displays the Top SQL for the selected time range. In real-time mode, the tab displays Top SQL only by DB time. In historical mode, the user can also display Top SQL by other metrics, such as CPU time or Executions.
- **RAC** -- Displays RAC-specific metrics such as the number of global cache blocks received, and the average block latency when the database is in a RAC configuration.
- **Monitored SQL** -- Displays Monitored Executions of SQL, PL/SQL and Database Operations in both real-time and historical mode.
- **ADDM** -- Displays ADDM and Automatic Real Time ADDM reports in both real-time and historical mode.
- **Current ADDM Findings** -- Displays a real-time analysis of system performance for the past 5 minutes. The tab is available only in real-time mode and the contents of this tab are populated only if the time selector includes the current time.

Composite Active Reports

A Composite Active Report is a single HTML file that embeds a set of correlated active reports. When viewing an active report, it is possible to navigate from one active report to another without requiring a connection to the database.

EM Cloud Control

Like EM Express, EM Cloud Control is a web-based tool for managing Oracle Database 12c. While, the similarity between the two does not end there, it certainly diverges rapidly. EM Cloud Control can do essentially everything that can be done in EM Express (with the exception of Composite Active Reports which have no Cloud Control equivalent). EM Cloud Control can perform dozens of functions that are not possible with EM Express.

Unlike EM Express, EM Cloud Control is Oracle's enterprise information technology management product and is completely separate from the Oracle 12c Database from a software standpoint. Enterprise Manager Cloud Control allows administrators to quickly set up, manage, and support enterprise clouds and traditional Oracle IT environments. It also provides the ability to manage the Oracle stack and engineered systems in real-time. Enterprise Manager Cloud Control is composed of the following components:

- **Oracle Management Agent** -- The Oracle Management Agent is deployed on each monitored host. It is responsible for monitoring the targets on those hosts, communicating that information to the middle-tier Oracle Management Service, and managing and maintaining the hosts and its targets.
- **Oracle Management Service** -- This service is a web-based application that works with the Management Agents and the Management Plug-ins to discover targets, monitor and manage those targets, and store the collected information in a repository. The service also renders the user interface for Enterprise Manager Cloud Control.
- **Oracle Management Repository** -- The Management Repository is a storage location where all of the information collected by the Management Agent is stored. It consists of objects such as database jobs, packages, procedures, views, and tablespaces.
- **Oracle Management Plug-ins** -- The core Enterprise Manager Cloud Control features for managing and monitoring Oracle technologies are now provided through plug-ins. These can be downloaded and deployed using the new Self Update feature.

This enables Cloud Control to be updated with management support for the latest Oracle product releases, without having to wait for the next Cloud Control release. The default plug-ins that are installed by default include:

- **Oracle Database** -- Enables you to monitor and manage Oracle Database and related targets such as Oracle Real Application Clusters (Oracle RAC), Oracle Automatic Storage Management (Oracle ASM), and so on.
- **Oracle Fusion Middleware** -- Enables you to monitor and manage Oracle Fusion Middleware products such as Oracle WebLogic Domain, Oracle WebLogic Cluster, etc.
- **My Oracle Support** -- Enables you to log in to My Oracle Support from within the Cloud Control console, search the knowledge library for notes and documents, raise service requests, and create patch plans and templates for patching monitored targets.
- **Oracle Exadata** -- Enables you to monitor and manage Oracle Exadata targets.

- **Enterprise Manager Cloud Control Console** -- The console is the user interface that you see after you install Enterprise Manager Cloud Control. With the help of the console, you can monitor and administer your entire computing environment from one location on the network. All the systems and services including enterprise application systems, databases, hosts, middleware application servers, listeners, and so on, are easily managed from one central location.

Manage structures used to undo changes made to the database and maintain data consistency

Whenever changes are made to the database, Oracle will simultaneously store the data that existed prior to the change. This is called undo or rollback data and is stored in the undo tablespace. When required, this information is used to undo changes to the database. Among other things, undo records are used to provide the following functionality:

- Roll back transactions when an implicit or explicit ROLLBACK is issued

- Recover after a failure
- Provide a read consistent view of the database
- Provide data from an earlier point in time using Oracle Flashback Query

When a ROLLBACK statement is issued, undo records are used to back out changes that were made to the database by the uncommitted transaction. If there is an abnormal shutdown of the database, during database recovery when the database is brought back up, the redo log will apply any data changes that did not make it to the datafiles. Then undo records are used to back out any uncommitted changes applied from the redo log to the datafiles. Read consistency is provided in the database by making use of the before image of the data that has been changed (but not committed). Users who access the data from rows that have been changed, but not committed will get their results back from the undo records rather than the changed information in the table record. With the undo records, multiple versions of the same data from different points in time can exist in the database. The database can make use of the undo log to generate snapshots of data at different points in time. Undo tablespaces can be associated with only a single instance, and each instance can have only a single undo tablespace writeable at a given time.

When automatic undo management is enabled, it has an undo retention period. This period is the minimum amount of time that the Database attempts to retain committed undo information before overwriting it. Any committed undo information that is older than retention period is considered to be expired, and a candidate to be overwritten. Committed undo information that is less than the retention period is unexpired and Oracle attempts to retain it for consistent read and Oracle Flashback operations. It is also possible to guarantee the retention period by enabling RETENTION GUARANTEE for the undo tablespace. If this is enabled, Oracle will never overwrite expired transactions that are more recent than the guaranteed period even if this means that new transactions will fail for lack of undo space.

Oracle will automatically tune the undo retention period based on the undo tablespace size and system activity. Alternately, you can explicitly set a minimum undo retention period with the UNDO_RETENTION initialization parameter. However, the UNDO_RETENTION parameter is ignored for a fixed size undo tablespace unless retention guarantee is enabled.

Managing the UNDO Tablespace

Starting with Oracle 11g, automatic undo management became the default during database creation. DBCA automatically creates an auto-extending undo tablespace named UNDOTBS1. During startup, the database will automatically use the first available undo tablespace for undo records. If no undo tablespace is available, the instance will store undo records in the SYSTEM tablespace. This is not recommended and a warning will be written to the alert log file that the system is running without an undo tablespace. If the database contains multiple undo tablespaces, it is possible to specify at startup for a specific undo tablespace to be used. This is done by setting the UNDO_TABLESPACE initialization parameter:

```
UNDO_TABLESPACE = undotbs_01
```

While DBCA automatically creates an undo tablespace during the installation process, it is possible to manually create additional undo tablespaces if required. However, while a database can contain multiple undo tablespaces, only one can be active at any given time. Also, database objects cannot be created in an undo tablespace. They are reserved for system-managed undo data.

Undo tablespaces can be created by two different methods. The first creates an undo tablespace when the CREATE DATABASE statement is issued. This occurs when a new database is created and the instance is started in automatic undo management mode (UNDO_MANAGEMENT =

AUTO). The second method allows you to create an undo tablespace in an existing database and uses the CREATE UNDO TABLESPACE statement. Oracle determines most attributes of the undo tablespace, but it is possible to specify the DATAFILE clause. The following example creates the undotbs_02 undo tablespace with the AUTOEXTEND option:

```
CREATE UNDO TABLESPACE undotbs_02
DATAFILE '/u02/oracle/ocp_db1/undo0201.dbf' SIZE 4M REUSE AUTOEXTEND
ON;
```

Undo tablespaces can be altered using the ALTER TABLESPACE statement. Most aspects of undo tablespaces are system managed, so only the following options can be altered:

- Adding a data file
- Renaming a data file
- Bringing a data file online or taking it offline
- Beginning or ending an open backup on a data file
- Enabling and disabling undo retention guarantee

The following example adds another data file to undo tablespace undotbs_01:

```
ALTER TABLESPACE undotbs_01
ADD DATAFILE '/u02/oracle/ocp_db1/undo0102.dbf' AUTOEXTEND ON NEXT 1M
MAXSIZE UNLIMITED;
```

The DROP TABLESPACE statement can be used to drop an undo tablespace. An undo tablespace can only be dropped if it is not currently used by any instance. If the tablespace contains any outstanding transactions, the DROP statement will fail. The following example drops the undo tablespace undotbs_02:

```
DROP TABLESPACE undotbs_02;
```

It is possible to switch from using one undo tablespace to another using the ALTER SYSTEM SET statement. The database is online during the switch operation, and user transactions can be in process while the command is executed. If the switch operation completes successfully, all transactions started after the switch operation began will be assigned to transaction tables in the new undo tablespace. If there are any pending transactions in the previous undo tablespace, it enters into a PENDING OFFLINE mode. While in this mode, existing transactions can continue to execute, but undo records for new transactions will not be stored in this undo tablespace. The following statement switches to a new undo tablespace:

```
ALTER SYSTEM SET UNDO_TABLESPACE = undotbs_02;
```

If the parameter value for UNDO TABLESPACE is set to '' (two single quotes), then the current undo tablespace is switched out and the next available undo tablespace is switched in. Use this statement with care because there may be no undo tablespace available.

```
ALTER SYSTEM SET UNDO_TABLESPACE = '';
```

Administering Users and Security

Create and administer users

The data in an Oracle database cannot be accessed without a connection to the database. In order to make a connection to the database, it is necessary to supply a valid database user name. Oracle user names are established by database administrators, and information about the user is stored in the data dictionary. The CREATE USER statement allows you to add new user accounts to an Oracle database. In order to create a user, you must have the CREATE USER system privilege. This is a powerful privilege, and is normally restricted to a database administrator or security administrator. The various elements that should be defined when creating a user are:

- **USERNAME** – User names in a database must be unique. They also share a namespace with roles, which means that you cannot have an identical username and role in a single database. When a user is created in a database, an associated schema is created of the same name.
- **AUTHENTICATION** – In order to connect to the database, each user must be authenticated. Most commonly, the connecting user must supply the correct password to the database in order to connect. The IDENTIFIED BY clause in the CREATE USER statement is used to specify a password.
- **DEFAULT TABLESPACE** – Each user should have a default tablespace. When a user creates a schema object and the DDL statement does not specify a tablespace, the user's default tablespace is where it will be created. If not specified, the default tablespaces for a user will be the SYSTEM tablespace. SYSTEM is a <u>terrible</u> place for users to create objects. For any user that will be creating objects, you should assign a default tablespace other than SYSTEM. It is also possible to change the default tablespace used by Oracle from SYSTEM to another tablespace. The database will automatically reassign to the new default tablespace all non-SYSTEM users. All objects subsequently created by those users will by default be stored in the tablespace.
- **QUOTA** – By default, users have no quota on any tablespace in the database. A quota grants users a set amount of space for

objects in a given tablespace. For users that will be creating objects in the database, you should assign a quota to them. During user creation, you can assign a quota to a single tablespace (presumably their default tablespace) or to more than one tablespaces by repeating the quota line.

- **TEMPORARY TABLESPACE** – Users need to make use of a temporary tablespace when performing operations that create temporary segments. Temporary segments are created by the system when performing sort or join operations.
- **PROFILE** – A profile is a set of limits on database resources and password access to the database. If you do not specify a profile, then Oracle Database assigns the user a default profile.

The following CREATE USER statement combines all of the elements described above to create a user with a password, default and temporary tablespaces, quota on two tablespaces, and a profile:

```
CREATE USER ocpuser
IDENTIFIED BY dumbpassword
DEFAULT TABLESPACE user_ts
QUOTA 10M ON test_ts
QUOTA 50M ON user_ts
TEMPORARY TABLESPACE temp_ts
PROFILE geek;
```

A newly created user cannot connect to the database until the account has been granted the CREATE SESSION system privilege. As a general rule, immediately after creating a user account, an administrator will grant that to the user.

```
GRANT CREATE SESSION TO ocpuser;
```

Altering User Accounts

All of the above items, with the exception of the username, can be changed after the user account exists with the ALTER USER command. All of the options that can be changed by the ALTER USER command except one require the ALTER USER privilege. The exception is that any user can change their own password. The syntax for this is:

```
ALTER USER ocpuser IDENTIFIED BY alsodumbpassword;
```

As with the CREATE USER privilege, only database administrators or security administrators should have this system privilege. Allowing modifications to user accounts is an incredibly powerful and dangerous ability. Users with this privilege can change any user's password, or set tablespace quotas for a user on any tablespace in the database. You can use the ALTER USER statement to change individual values of a user, or multiple values at once, as in the following example:

```
ALTER USER ocpuser
IDENTIFIED EXTERNALLY
DEFAULT TABLESPACE data_ts
TEMPORARY TABLESPACE temp_ts
QUOTA 5M ON data_ts
PROFILE peon;
```

Predefined Administrative Accounts

There are two administrative accounts that are automatically created for every Oracle database:

- **SYS** – The user SYS is automatically created and granted the DBA role. All of the base tables and views for the database data dictionary are stored in the schema SYS. SYS is in effect the owner of the entire data dictionary. All of the tables and views in the data dictionary are critical to the function of Oracle Database. They should never be modified directly by anyone, and no tables should ever be created in the SYS schema. The SYS account should never be accessed by database users and administrators should avoid using it more than is absolutely necessary.
- **SYSTEM** – The user SYSTEM is also automatically created and granted the DBA role. The SYSTEM account is only slightly less critical to the functioning of the database than SYS. It is used to create tables and views that display administrative information, and internal tables and views used by various Oracle Database options and tools. As with SYS, the SYSTEM schema ideally should not be used to store non-standard objects of your own.

User account passwords are case sensitive by default. You can alter this behavior using the SEC_CASE_SENSITIVE_LOGON initialization parameter. Only users with the ALTER SYSTEM privilege can alter the value of this parameter. Set it to TRUE to enable case sensitivity or FALSE to disable case sensitivity. Oracle strongly recommends that you leave case sensitivity in passwords enabled.

Oracle supplies two new password complexity verification functions with 12c: ORA12C_VERIFY_FUNCTION and ORA12C_STRONG_VERIFY_FUNCTION. Either can be used as-is or modified as desired to provide improved password security for database accounts. The ORA12C_VERIFY_FUNCTION is similar to the VERIFY_FUNCTION_11G from the prior release with slightly stronger security. When implemented, it verifies the following when users attempt to change their password:

- Contains at least 8 characters
- Contains at least 1 letters
- Contains at least 1 digits
- Does not contain database name
- Does not contain user name or reverse user name
- Does not contain oracle
- Is not too simple (like welcome1)
- Differs by at least 3 characters from the old password

The ORA12C_STRONG_VERIFY_FUNCTION function provides stronger password complexity. It considers recommendations of the Department of Defense Database (STIG) with the following limits.

- Contains at least 9 characters
- Contains at least 2 capital letters
- Contains at least 2 small letters
- Contains at least 2 digits
- Contains at least 2 special characters
- Differs by at least 4 characters from the old password

You can customize either function to meet your own requirements. Oracle recommends that you do so, in fact. By default, password complexity verification is not enabled. To enable password complexity verification you must perform the following steps:

- Log in to SQL*Plus with administrative privileges and run the UTLPWDMG.SQL script (or your variant thereof) to create the password complexity function in the SYS schema.
- In the default profile or the user profile, set the PASSWORD_VERIFY_FUNCTION setting to either the sample password complexity function in the UTLPWDMG.SQL script, or to your customized function. Use one of the following methods:
  - ✓ Log in to SQL*Plus with administrator privileges and use the CREATE PROFILE or ALTER PROFILE statement to enable the function.

```
ALTER PROFILE default LIMIT
  PASSWORD_VERIFY_FUNCTION
  ora12c_strong_verify_function;
```

  - ✓ In Oracle Enterprise Manager, go to the Edit Profiles page and then under Complexity, select the name of the password complexity function from the complexity function list.

Oracle can make use of a cryptographic hashing algorithm based on SHA-1. This helps protect against password-based security threats by including support for mixed case characters, special characters, and multibyte characters in passwords. The SHA-1 hashing algorithm also adds salt to each password when it is hashed, which provides additional protection.

Grant privileges to users to perform database operations

There are two broad classes of privileges that can be granted to a user or role:

- **System Privileges** – Provide the ability to perform a task that has a scope beyond that of a single database object. Many of the system privileges have a scope of the entire database, for example ALTER USER or ALTER SYSTEM. Others have a scope that is just for the schema of the user who has been granted the privilege, for example CREATE TABLE or CREATE PROCEDURE.

- **Object Privileges** – Provide the ability to perform a task on a specific database object. For example, GRANT SELECT ON employees.

Some examples of System Privileges are:

- **CREATE TABLE** – Create a table in the grantee's schema.
- **CREATE ANY TABLE** – Create a table in any schema.
- **ALTER ANY TABLE** – Alter any table or view in any schema.
- **DELETE ANY TABLE** – Delete rows from tables in any schema.
- **DROP ANY TABLE** – Drop (or truncate) tables in any schema.
- **INSERT ANY TABLE** – Insert rows into tables in any schema.
- **CREATE ANY INDEX** – Create an index on any table in any schema.
- **ALTER ANY INDEX** – Alter indexes in any schema.

Some examples of Object Privileges are:

- **ALTER** – Right to use ALTER TABLE to change a given table.
- **INDEX** – Right to use the CREATE INDEX command on a given table.
- **INSERT** – Right to INSERT new rows into a given table.
- **SELECT** – Right to SELECT data from a given table.
- **UPDATE** – Right to UPDATE data in a given table.
- **DELETE** – Right to DELETE rows from a given table.

Administrator-Level System Privileges

There are several system privileges that provide an account with very high-level capabilities. These privileges should be granted rarely, and only to trusted users:

- **SYSDBA** – Allows a user to effectively connect as the SYS user. The account has full control over the database.
- **SYSOPER** – Allows a user to start up, shut down, and administer a database instance.

- **SYSASM** – Allows a user to start up, shut down, and administer an ASM instance.
- **RESTRICTED SESSION** – User can login when database is opened in restricted session mode.
- **ALTER DATABASE** – Allows a user to issue ALTER DATABASE commands.
- **ALTER SYSTEM** – Allows a user to issue ALTER SYSTEM commands.
- **GRANT ANY PRIVILEGE** – Allows a user to grant any system privilege to other accounts.
- **GRANT ANY OBJECT PRIVILEGE** – Allows a user to grant any privilege on objects in the database regardless of schema.

ANY keyword

A significant percentage of system privileges have two similar commands, with and without the ANY keyword (i.e. CREATE TABLE vs. CREATE ANY TABLE). The ANY keyword means that the grant is not schema-specific. When a user is granted CREATE TABLE, they are able to create tables in their own schema. However, when granted CREATE ANY TABLE, they can create tables in any user's schema. The ANY keyword makes the privilege much less restrictive and therefore much more dangerous.

WITH ADMIN OPTION

System privileges may optionally be made using the WITH ADMIN option (i.e. GRANT ALTER ANY TABLE WITH ADMIN OPTION). This option allows the user granted this privilege to grant it to other users in turn. In fact, they can grant the privilege to a third user 'WITH ADMIN OPTION' who could in turn grant it to a fourth and so on. If the system privilege is later revoked from a user who was given the admin option, any grants they made of this system privilege are not revoked. The revoke of system privileges <u>does not</u> cascade.

WITH GRANT OPTION

Object privileges have a similar clause called the WITH GRANT OPTION. When an object privilege is granted to a user with this option, that user can grant the object privilege to other users. One distinct difference between the two is that if the privilege is revoked from a user given the WITH GRANT OPTION, any privileges that the user granted are also revoked. The revoke of object privileges does cascade.

Grant privileges on tables

In order to access tables that are owned by another schema, you must have been granted the privileges to do so. This might be through a system privilege such as SELECT ANY TABLE, or by a grant on the table itself by the schema owner, or another database user that has privileges that allow them to grant the required access. Until a privilege has been granted, Oracle will treat attempts to access it as if the table does not even exist.

```
SELECT *
FROM   hr.regions;

ORA-00942: table or view does not exist
00942. 00000 -  "table or view does not exist"
```

If the SELECT privilege is granted to the querying schema, then the above statement will succeed:

```
GRANT SELECT ON hr.regions TO ocpguru;
GRANT succeeded.

SELECT *
FROM   hr.regions;

REGION_ID REGION_NAME
----- -------------
        1 Europe
        2 Americas
        3 Asia
        4 Middle East and Africa
```

To remove a privilege that has been granted, the REVOKE statement is required:

```
REVOKE SELECT ON hr.regions FROM ocpguru;

REVOKE succeeded.
```

QUOTAS

Users who will be creating objects need to be assigned a quota on the tablespace(s) where those objects will be created. On account creation, users will have zero quota on all tablespaces by default. Quota allows users to consume a limited amount of space in a designated location. There is no need to grant users quota on temporary tablespaces or on undo tablespaces.

If at some point you alter a user's quota to be less than their previous one, then the following rules apply:

- If the new tablespace quota has already been exceeded, existing objects cannot be allocated more space until their combined space is less than the new quota.
- If the new quota has not been exceeded, then the user's objects can be allocated space up to the new quota.

The alternative to granting a quota to a user is granting the UNLIMITED TABLESPACE privilege. However, in that case, you have lost control over how much space the user account can consume and which tablespace it will be used in. Quota is a much more controlled means of giving users access to space. The UNLIMITED TABLESPACE privilege overrides all explicit tablespace quotas for the user. If you later revoke the privilege, then you must explicitly grant quotas to individual tablespaces. You can grant this privilege only to users, not to roles.

Create and manage roles

A role is a container for a set of privileges. It is not in and of itself a privilege. When created, a new role contains no privileges and granting it to a user would confer no additional rights within the database. Once privileges have been added to a role and the role granted to a user, the user can then enable it and exercise the privileges granted to it. A default role is automatically enabled for a user when the user creates a session. You can assign a user zero or more default roles.

Privileges granted to a schema are part of that schema even when the user is not logged in to the database. By contrast, the privileges a schema has from a role are only in effect while the user has an open database session and the role is enabled. Non-default roles must be enabled manually by issuing the SET ROLE command. Non-default roles can be password protected by adding the IDENTIFIED BY clause when creating the role.

Both system and object privileges can be granted to roles and those roles subsequently granted to users. Roles are useful for quickly and easily granting multiple permissions to users. There are also a number of roles that have been pre-defined by Oracle. You can grant these roles to users if you wish. However, Oracle recommends creating your own roles that contain only the privileges pertaining to your requirements so that you have more control. Oracle has been known to change the privileges in pre-defined roles. They did so with the CONNECT role, which originally had nine privileges, but now only has the CREATE SESSION privilege.

```
CREATE ROLE hr_authority;
role HR_AUTHORITY created.

GRANT SELECT ON employees TO hr_authority;
GRANT succeeded.

GRANT UPDATE ON employees TO hr_authority;
GRANT succeeded.

GRANT DELETE ON employees TO hr_authority;
GRANT succeeded.
```

```
GRANT hr_authority to jjones;
GRANT succeeded.
```

Predefined Roles

- **CONNECT** – Has the CONNECT SESSION privilege.
- **RESOURCE** – Has privileges that allows users to create tables, indexes, triggers, sequences and more in their own schema. Prior to release 12c, this role also provided the UNLIMITED TABLESPACE privilege to the user.
- **DBA** – This role contains the vast majority of database system privileges. The DBA role should be granted only to actual database administrators.
- **SELECT_CATALOG_ROLE** – Allows a user to view the data dictionary but does not allow viewing of data.
- **SCHEDULER_ADMIN** – Provides the system privileges required to manage the Oracle Scheduler.
- **PUBLIC** – Every user has this role. It is a placeholder where you can grant privileges that should be available to every user in the database. After granting a privilege to PUBLIC, the privilege is freely available to every single database user without exception. This must always be used with caution, especially when dealing with system privileges.

There are three new roles in Oracle 12c for database administrative activities, including backup and recovery, high availability, and key management. The new roles eliminate the need to grant the SYSDBA role for common day-to-day operations.

- **SYSBACKUP** -- This allows Recovery Manager (RMAN) users to connect to the target database and run RMAN commands.
- **SYSDG** -- The SYSDG administrative privilege is used to perform Data Guard operations. This privilege can be used with either Data Guard Broker or the DGMGRL command-line interface. In order to connect to the database as SYSDG using a password, you must create a password file for it.

- **SYSKM** -- The SYSKM administrative privilege enables the SYSKM user to manage Transparent Data Encryption wallet operations. In order to connect to the database as SYSKM using a password, you must create a password file for it.

Software Installation and Maintenance

Install the Oracle database software

The installation of the Oracle Database is a reasonably involved process and until you have done it a few times, the best bet is to have the installation manual for the proper OS open in your browser and to follow it step-by-step as you work. This chapter will cover some of the highlights of installing Oracle 12c on Oracle Linux 6. Before making any changes to the destination system, first check to ensure it meets the minimum requirements for installing Oracle 12c:

The disk space requirements for the software files (*not* the database files) on Linux x86-64 are:

- Enterprise Edition: 6.4 GB
- Standard Edition: 6.1 GB
- Standard Edition One: 6.1 GB

The memory requirements for installing Oracle Database 12c under Linux is 1 GB but 2 or more GB is recommended. The amount of swap space recommended depends on the amount or RAM in the system.

- For systems with 1-2 GB of ram, swap space should be 150% of the RAM.
- For systems with 2-16 GB of ram, swap space should be equal to the RAM.
- For systems with >16 GB of ram, swap space should be 16GB.

Once it has been determined that a system can host Oracle 12c, there are a number of pre-installation tasks that must be performed on a Linux server before running the Oracle installer. The complete list is in the Oracle installation manual for Linux. However, if you are running Oracle Linux 6, there is an Oracle RDBMS Server pre-install RPM package available. This package makes it much easier to install the Oracle

Database. The package will perform most of the pre-install configuration tasks automatically. Among other things, it creates the 'oracle' user and the groups needed for Oracle Database installation. It also modifies kernel parameters in /etc/sysctl.conf and resource limits in /etc/security/limits.conf. It also ensures that several packages required by Oracle are installed on the system. This significantly reduces the amount of time required to prepare the server before installing Oracle. The following command will download and install the RPM and prepare your OL6 system for the Oracle install:

```
yum install oracle-rdbms-server-12cR1-preinstall
```

Download the installation files from Oracle. For 64-bit Linux, there are two files, **linuxamd64_12c_database_1of2** and **linuxamd64_12c_database_2of2**. These should be placed into the /tmp directory of your Linux server and then extracted in place as the oracle user with the unzip command:

```
[oracle@ocp tmp]unzip linuxamd64_12c_database_1of2.zip
...
[oracle@ocp tmp]unzip linuxamd64_12c_database_2of2.zip
...
```

Once the files are unzipped, change to the /tmp/database directory and run the Oracle installer:

```
[oracle@ocp database] ./runInstaller
```

If everything has been configured correctly, executing the installer should get you to the 'Configure Security Updates' screen of the Oracle 12c installation.

Step 1: Configure Security Updates -- In this screen, you will provide an email address where Oracle can inform you of security issues with the database. Optionally, you can opt to receive security updates via My Oracle Support.

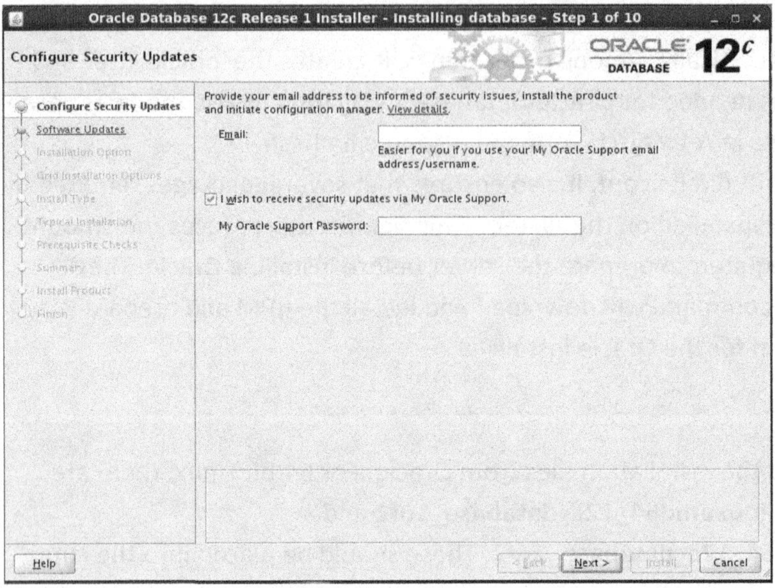

Step 2: Download Software Updates -- You can opt to download software updates via My Oracle Support if you have an account. Optionally, you can choose to use pre-downloaded updates or skip the software updates entirely.

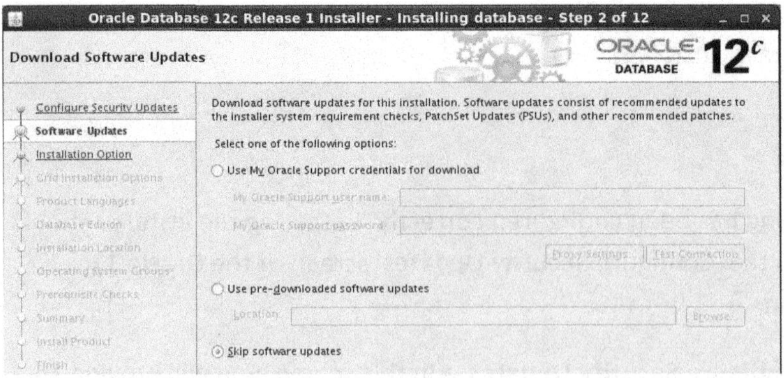

Step 3: Installation Option -- In this step you can choose to install the Oracle software and create a database, just install the software, or upgrade an existing software installation.

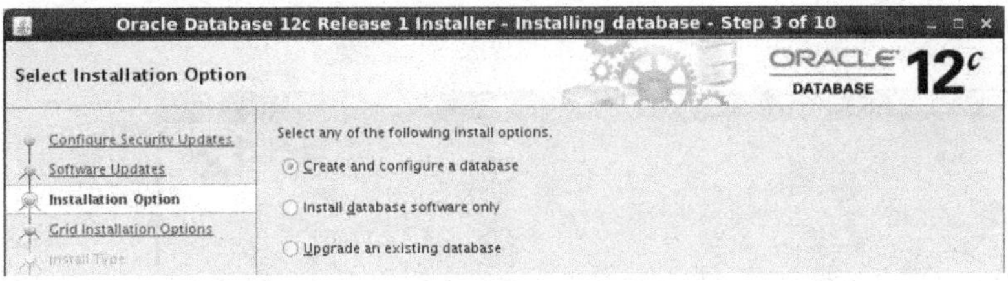

Step 4: Grid Installation Options -- This screen allows you to select between a single instance database installation, Oracle Real Application Clusters database installation, or Oracle RAC One Node database installation.

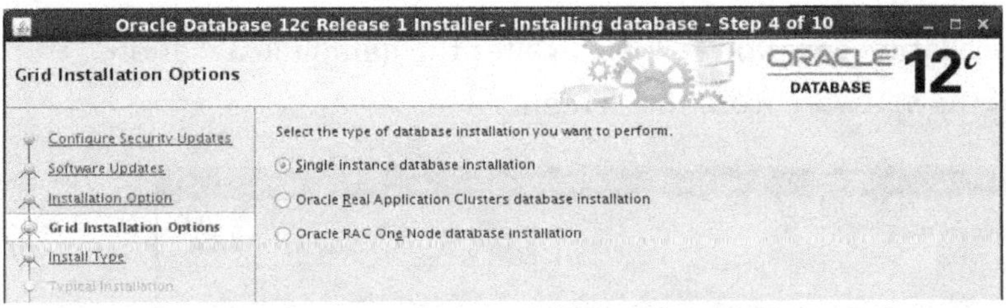

Step 5: Product Language -- In this screen you can add additional languages to the Oracle database installation.

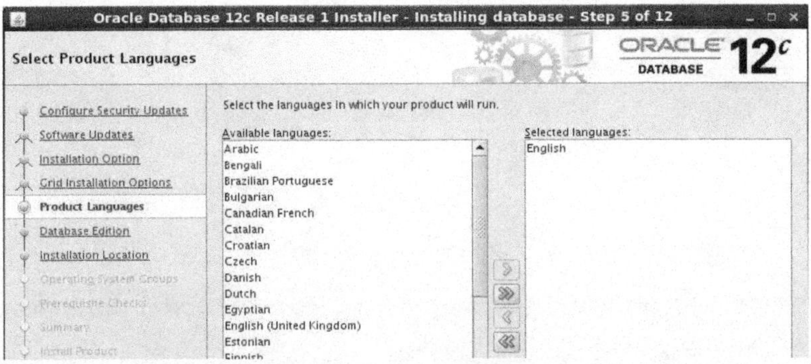

Step 6: Database Edition -- In this screen, you must select between installation the Oracle Enterprise, Standard Edition, or Standard Edition One product versions.

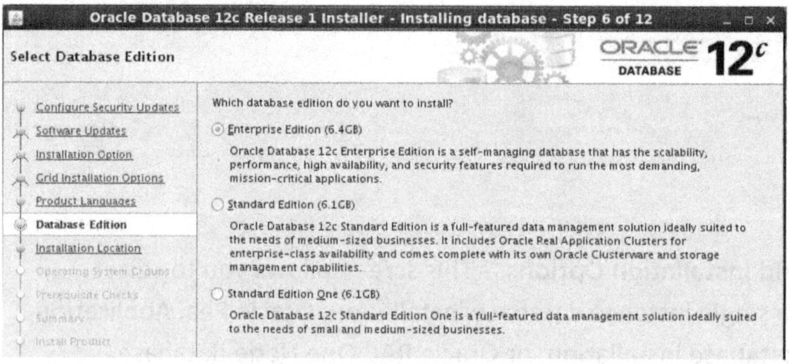

Step 7: Installation Location -- You can alter the default installation location of the software from this screen.

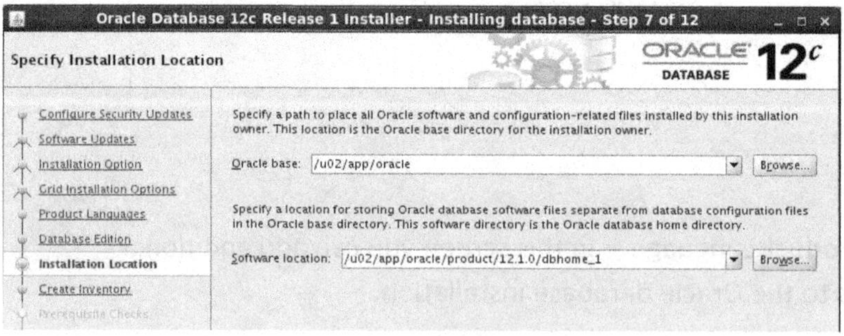

Step 8: Create Inventory -- This screen determines the locations to store the installation metadata files.

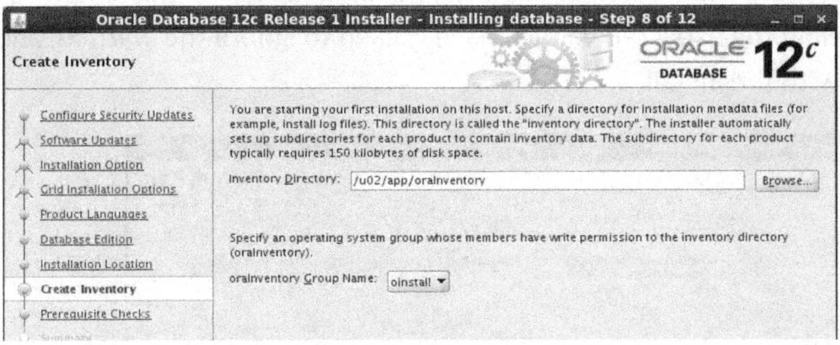

Step 9: Operating System Groups -- In this screen, operating system groups are mapped to database privileges.

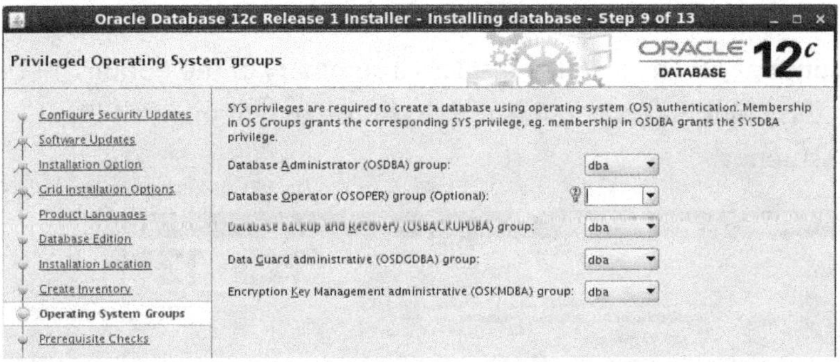

Step 10: Prerequisite Checks -- The installer verifies that all of the prerequisites for an Oracle installation have been met. If any checks fail, they are listed in the screen. In this case, the swap space on the system is slightly below the expected value. I have clicked to ignore the warning and move on with the install.

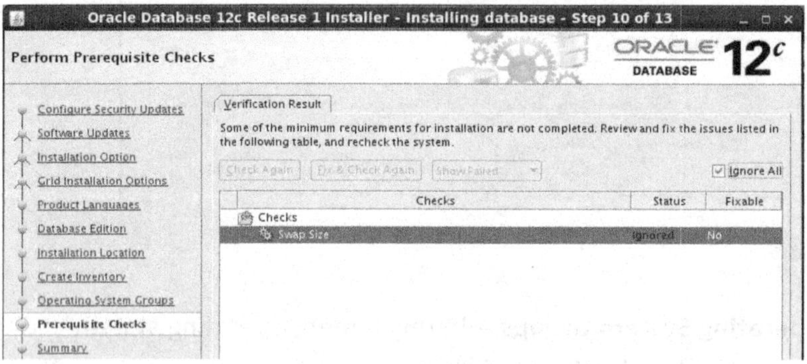

Step 11: Summary -- The installer displays a summary of the options chosen to this point in the install. You can choose to edit many of them from this screen.

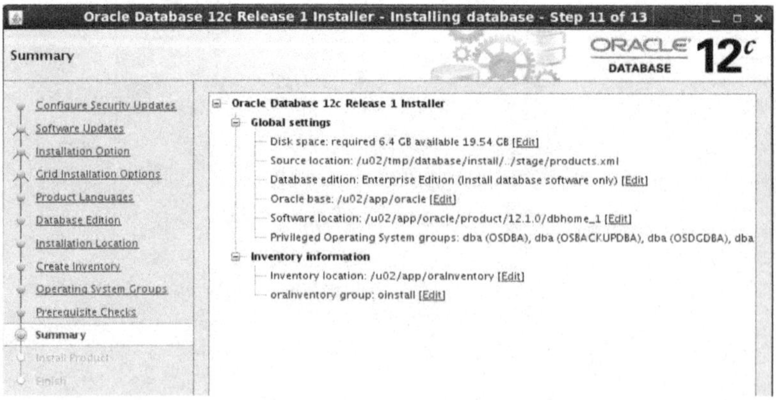

Step 12: Install Product -- In this screen, the installer performs the file copy and other installation tasks.

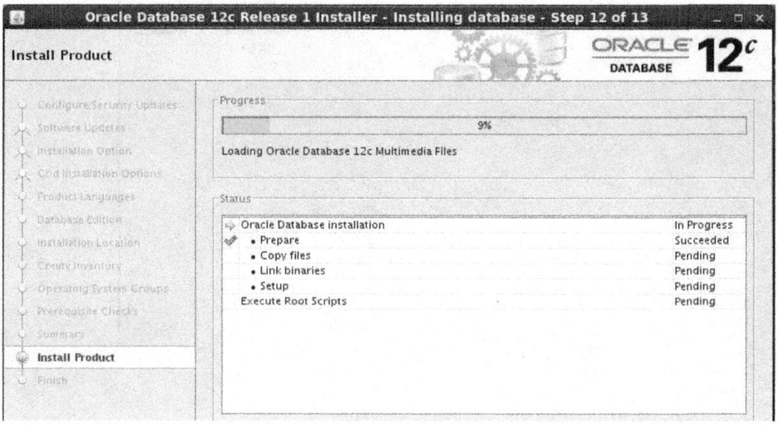

Step 12a: Root Scripts -- The final step of the installation requires two scripts to be run as the root user.

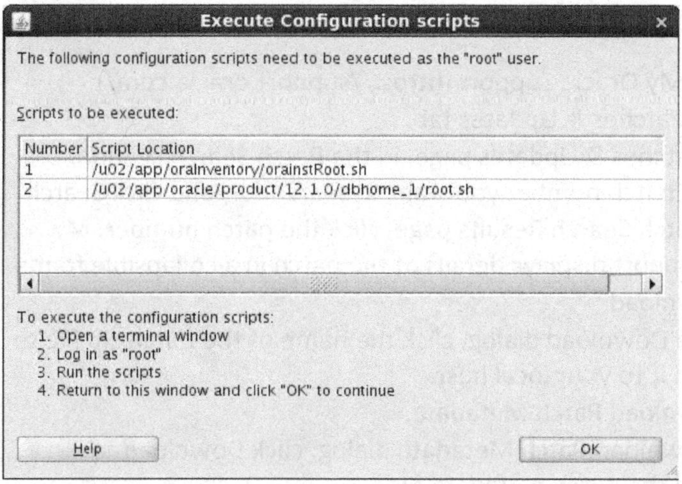

Step 13: Finish -- This is the screen you really want to see.

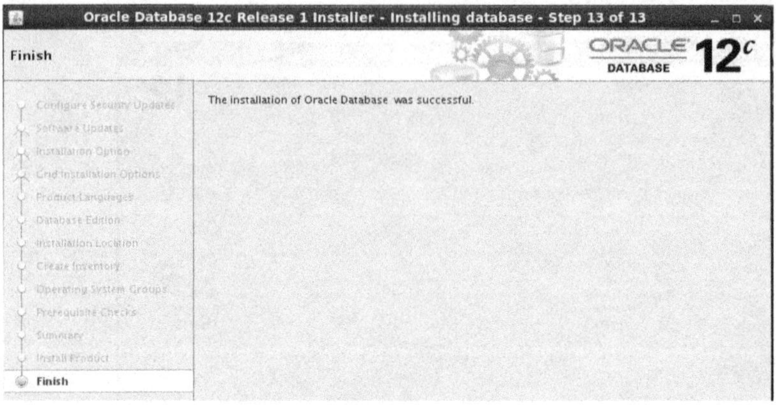

Locate patches for the Oracle database

You can locate patches and their metadata files at the My Oracle support website. The steps to do this are:

- Log in to My Oracle Support (https://support.oracle.com/)
- Click the Patches & Updates tab
- On the Patches & Updates page, in the Patch Search section, enter the patch number you want to search for, and click Search.
- On the Patch Search Results page, click the patch number. My Oracle Support displays details of the patch in a collapsible frame.
- Click Download.
- In the File Download dialog, click the name of the patch zip file to download it to your local host.
- Click Download Patch Metadata.
- In the Download Patch Metadata dialog, click Download to download the patch metadata file.

Enterprise Manager Cloud Control

For patching targets in Enterprise Manager Cloud Control in offline mode, the patches and their metadata files must already have been stored in Software Library so that they can be searched, selected, and added to the patch plans. Once the above process is used to obtain the files, they must be uploaded to the Software Library.

When using Enterprise Manager Cloud control in Online mode, it is possible to search for (and apply) patches directly from the Cloud Control interface.

Apply best practices to patching the database

After installation and on a regular basis, DBAs should download and install patches to the Oracle software. There are several varieties of patches produced by Oracle, including:

- **Interim Patches** -- These contain a single bug fix or a collection of bug fixes provided as required. They may also be one-offs for customer-specific security bug fixes.
- **Diagnostic Patches** -- These are intended to help diagnose or verify a fix or a collection of bug fixes.
- **Patch Set Updates (PSU)** -- These contain a collection of high impact, low risk, and proven fixes for a specific product or component.
- **Security Patch Updates** -- These contain a cumulative collection of security bug fixes.
- **Critical Patch Updates (CPU)** -- These contain a collection of security bug fixes.

Some patches can be installed while the database is running using either OPatch or the Enterprise Manager Patch Wizard (which uses opatch in the background). You can determine what patches are applicable to your system through the Patch Advisor in Enterprise Manager Cloud Control.

Online Patches

Prior to release 11g of Oracle, all patches contained .o (object) files and/or .a (archive) libraries. Installing them required a relink of the RDBMS binary and therefore meant the database had to be shut down before the patch could be applied. Now an increasingly large number of patches are available as online patches. These contain .so files, which are dynamic/shared libraries, and they do not require a relink of the RDBMS binary. Because a relink is not needed, online patches can be applied or rolled back while the database instance is running. This simplifies administration, because no downtime is needed. It also means that installing or de-installing Online Patches is faster – potentially taking just a few seconds. Online patches will be installed using the opatch utility.

The benefits of online patches include the following:

- No downtime is required
- They persist across shutdowns
- They allow rolling patches in RAC
- They have a fast installation

There are few downsides to online patches:

- They require more memory
- Online patching isn't available on all platforms
- Not all patches are available as hot patches

EM Cloud Control

Oracle Enterprise Manager Cloud Control 12c has a new patch management capability that reduces the difficulty and downtime associated with patching the database. The new patch management solution offers the following benefits:

- Integrated patching workflow with My Oracle Support. A single interface allows you to see recommendations, search for patches, and roll out patches.
- Patch plans allow for end-to-end orchestration of the patching workflow. Plans include including automated selection of deployment procedures and analysis of the patch conflicts.
- Easy review of patches for applicability to a given environment, validation of patch plans, and automatic receipt of patches to resolve validation issues.
- Deployable patch plans can be saved as patch templates, which contain a predetermined set of patches and deployment options.
- Out-of-place patching is possible for standalone database targets, Oracle Real Application Clusters (RAC) targets, and Oracle Grid Infrastructure targets.

Cloud Control patch plans help you create a consolidated list of patches you want to apply as a group to one or more targets. A patch can be added to a target in a plan only if the patch has the same release and platform as the target to which it is being added. The plan also validates Oracle Database, Fusion Middleware, and Cloud Control patches against the environment to check for conflicts with installed patches. Based on the patches added to it, Enterprise Manager automatically selects an appropriate deployment procedure to be used for applying the patches.

EM Cloud Control can apply patches in two different modes:

- **Online Mode** -- This mode is useful when Cloud Control can connect to My Oracle Support using an Internet connection. This mode allows administrators to see recommendations from Oracle for the patches to be applied, manually search patches directly on My Oracle Support and add them to a patch plan. It is also possible to automatically resolve patch conflicts with a merge patch directly from My Oracle Support.
- **Offline Mode** -- This mode is used when Cloud Control cannot connect to My Oracle Support. In this mode, it is only possible to search for patches that were manually uploaded to the Software Library, and add them to your patch plan.

Queryable Patch Inventory

Oracle 12c introduces a new feature called the Queryable Patch Inventory. This feature is implemented via the DBMS_QOPATCH package. It provides a PL/SQL or SQL interface to view the patches that are installed in the database. The interface provides all the patch information available as part of the OPatch lsinventory -xml command. DBMS_QOPATCH accesses the Oracle Universal Installer (OUI) patch inventory in real time to provide patch and patch meta information. With this feature, it is possible to:

- Query what patches are installed from a SQL prompt.
- Create reports and perform validation checks across multiple environments.
- Check patches installed on Oracle RAC nodes from a single location.

The subprograms available in the DBMS_QOPATCH include:

- **GET_OPATCH_BUGS** -- Provides a bugs list for a patch in XML format if the patch number is given. If patch is not given then it lists all the bugs installed in all the patches in XML format.
- **GET_OPATCH_COUNT** -- Provides the total number of installed patches in XML format.
- **GET_OPATCH_DATA** -- Provides top level patch information for the patch (such as Patch ID, patch creation time) in the XML element.
- **GET_OPATCH_FILES** -- Provides the list of files modified in the given patch number in XML format.
- **GET_OPATCH_INSTALL_INFO** -- Returns the XML element containing the ORACLE_HOME details such as patch and inventory location.
- **GET_OPATCH_LIST** -- Provides list of patches installed as an XML element from the XML inventory.
- **GET_OPATCH_LSINVENTORY** -- Returns whole opatch inventory as XML instance document.
- **GET_OPATCH_OLAYS** -- Provides overlay patches for a given patch as XML element.

- **GET_OPATCH_PREQS** -- Provides prerequisite patches for a given patch as XML element.
- **GET_OPATCH_XSLT** -- Returns the style-sheet for the opatch XML inventory presentation.
- **GET_PENDING_ACTIVITY** -- Returns the information related to SQL patches applied on a single instance by querying the binary inventory.
- **GET_SQLPATCH_STATUS** -- Displays the SQL patch status by querying from SQL patch registry to produce complete patch level information.
- **IS_PATCH_INSTALLED** -- Provides information (such as patchID, application date, and SQL patch information) on the installed patch as XML node by querying the XML inventory
- **PATCH_CONFLICT_DETECTION** -- Returns the conflicting patch for a given file, if it conflicts with an existing patch
- **SET_CURRENT_OPINST** -- Sets the node name and instance to get the inventory details specific to it in an Oracle Real Application Clusters (RAC) environment

Apply troubleshooting tasks for planned database maintenance

Planned database maintenance windows have historically required the advance scheduling of planned downtime in order to provide a window where the database will be unavailable to users. Maintenance windows are used to backup the database, replace or add hardware components, upgrade or patch software, and so on. To provide maximum availability of the database, the need for downtime must be minimized. Oracle 12c has numerous capabilities designed to allow for routine maintenance tasks to be performed on the database without making the data unavailable to users and applications. Many maintenance operations can now be made while the database itself continues to be available. Other maintenance operations can be performed in a rolling fashion using a synchronized copy of the production database. The capabilities available in Oracle 12c to allow for this include:

- **Hot Patching** -- Online patching through the OPatch utility provides the ability to patch the processes in an Oracle instance without having to bring it down. When performing online patching, each process associated with the instance will check for patched code at a safe execution point, and copy the new code into its process space.
- **Rolling Patch Upgrades using Oracle RAC** -- Patches can be applied to the nodes of a Real Application Cluster (RAC) system in a rolling fashion. A rolling upgrade is performed by quiesing and patching one of the instances while the other instance(s) in the server pool continue in service. The process is repeated until all instances are patched. The rolling upgrade is applicable to all patch types (Patch Set Updates (PSUs), Critical Patch Updates (CPUs), one-off database and diagnostic patches) as well as operating system upgrades and hardware changes.
- **Data Guard Standby-First Patch Assurance** -- This capability allows a physical standby database to support different software patch levels between a primary and standby database. This allows for Oracle patches to be applied and validated in a rolling fashion.
- **Rolling Upgrades using Active Data Guard** -- Three PL/SQL packages that are part of the Active Data Guard package automate much of the process of performing a rolling upgrade between a Data Guard primary and physical standby database.
- **Online System Reconfiguration** -- Oracle's Automatic Storage Management (ASM) has built-in capabilities that allow the ASM disks to be added or removed while a Diskgroup remains online. When disks are added or removed from an ASM Diskgroup, the data is automatically rebalanced for the new storage configuration without affecting access to the data. When using a Real Application Clusters (RAC) configuration, administrators can dynamically add and remove clustered nodes without any disruption to the database or the application.
- **Online Data File Move** -- Oracle Database 12c has the ability to move a data file while users are accessing its data, via command ALTER DATABASE MOVE DATAFILE. This capability maintains data availability during maintenance operations.
- **Online Partition Move** -- Oracle 12c now supports online, multi-partition redefinition in a single session.

- **Online Table Redefinition** -- The DBMS_REDEFINITION package can be used to reduce downtime by allowing changes to a table structure while continuing to allow access to the original structure, including insert/update/delete operations. The maintenance process modifies an interim copy of the table and then synchronizes it with the original. Once the maintenance procedures are complete, the administrator performs the final synchronization and activates the newly structured table.
- **Online Application Upgrades: Edition-Based Redefinition** -- This capability allows the online upgrade of an application without interrupting its availability. Once the installation of the upgrade is complete, the pre-upgrade application and the post-upgrade application can be used at the same time. Existing sessions can continue to use the pre-upgrade application, while all new sessions use the post-upgrade application. The application as a whole enjoys hot rollover from the pre-upgrade version to the post-upgrade version.
- **Zero Downtime Maintenance using Oracle GoldenGate** -- GoldenGate logical replication is able to keep databases on different platforms or versions synchronized. With this capability, changes to be implemented on a copy of a production database and then synchronized with the old version. Once validated, users are switched to the copy running at the new version or on the new platform.

View and modify the parameters used to configure the Oracle instance

When an Oracle instance starts, it makes use of an initialization parameter file to determine many of the database settings that will be used. At minimum, this file must specify the DB_NAME parameter. If the file contains nothing else, all other parameters will be set to default values. There are two types of parameter file that Oracle can use: a text-based parameter file that is read-only to the Oracle instance (PFILE), or a binary file that the instance can both read from and write to (SPFILE). When an instance stats, Oracle uses the following steps to locate an initialization parameter file. It will use the first file it locates:

1. It looks for spfile[SID].ora
2. It looks for spfile.ora
3. It looks for init[SID].ora

The recommended option is to utilize the binary file. It is called a server parameter file or spfile. Unlike the text-based file, with a spfile, you can change initialization parameters using ALTER SYSTEM commands and have those changes persist across a database shutdown and startup. The spfile also provides a method by which Oracle can self-tune. A spfile can be created manually from your text-based initialization file. Alternately, DBCA can automatically generate one when the database is created. When a server parameter file does not exist, the instance will start using a text initialization parameter file. At startup, the instance initially searches for a server parameter file in a default location. Only if it does not find one will the instance will search for a text initialization parameter file. It's also possible to bypass an existing server parameter file by naming a PFILE as a STARTUP argument.

The default file name for the text initialization parameter file is init[SID].ora. For a database with a SID of oraprod, the default filename would be initoraprod.ora. The default location under Unix and Linux is in the ORACLE_HOME/dbs directory. Under MS Windows, the file would be stored in ORACLE_HOME\database by default.

Many of the database initialization parameters can be dynamically changed using the ALTER SYSTEM statement. For instances using a spfile, such changes can persist across shutdowns. However, if you are using a text initialization parameter file, any changes made via ALTER SYSTEM are effective only for the current instance. You must update them manually in the initialization parameter file to make them permanent.

The text initialization parameter file contains name/value pairs in one of the following forms:

- **Single-Value Parameters** – parameter_name=value
- **Multiple-Value Parameters** – parameter_name=(value[,value] ...)

Multiple-value parameters can also be entered on multiple lines using the same format as a single parameter. If a single-value parameter appears on more than one line in the file, only the last value will be used.

Some initialization parameters derive their values from the values of other parameters. As a general rule, the values for derived parameters should not be altered. However, if they are explicitly set, then the specified value will override the calculated value. An example of a derived parameter is SESSIONS. This parameter is calculated from the value of the PROCESSES parameter. Unless SESSIONS is set explicitly, when the value of PROCESSES changes, then the default value of SESSIONS changes as well.

The host operating system will determine the valid values or value ranges of some initialization parameters. The DB_BLOCK_BUFFERS parameter indicates the number of data buffers in main memory. The maximum allowable value for this parameter depends on the operating system. In addition, the size of data block buffers, set by DB_BLOCK_SIZE, defaults to 8K under most operating systems.

Common Initialization Parameters

The following are all commonly set initialization parameters. These and other initialization parameters are listed in more detail in the Oracle 12c Reference Manual.

- **DB_NAME** – Determines the local component of the database name.
- **DB_DOMAIN** – Indicates the domain (logical location) within a network structure. This parameter is optional. The combination of the DB_NAME and DB_DOMAIN must create a database name that is unique within a network.
- **CONTROL_FILES** – Specifies one or more control filenames for the database. Control files are generated at the time a database is created using the names specified by the CONTROL_FILES parameter. If you do not include CONTROL_FILES in the

initialization parameter file, Oracle will create a control file in the same directory as the initialization parameter file, using a default operating system–dependent filename.

- **PROCESSES** – Determines the maximum number of OS processes that can connect to Oracle simultaneously. At minimum, this parameter must have a minimum value of one for each background process plus one for each user process.
- **MEMORY_TARGET** – Sets a target memory size for the instance. The total memory used by the instance will remain reasonably constant, based on the supplied value. The instance will automatically distribute memory between the system global area (SGA) and the instance program global area (instance PGA).
- **SGA_TARGET** – If MEMORY_TARGET is not set, you can enable the automatic shared memory management feature by setting the SGA_TARGET parameter to a nonzero value. This parameter sets the total size of the SGA. Oracle will automatically tune the SGA components as needed.
- **SGA_MAX_SIZE** – Specifies the maximum size of the System Global Area for the lifetime of the instance. If you do not specify SGA_MAX_SIZE, then Oracle Database selects a default value that is the sum of all components specified or defaulted at the time of initialization.
- **PGA_AGGREGATE_TARGET** – Allows you to control the total amount of memory dedicated to the instance PGA.
- **UNDO_MANAGEMENT** – When set to AUTO or null, this parameter enables automatic undo management. When set to MANUAL, undo management will use manual mode.
- **UNDO_TABLESPACE** – This parameter is optional, and valid only in automatic undo management mode. The parameter specifies the name of an undo tablespace. It is used only when the database has multiple undo tablespaces.
- **DB_BLOCK_SIZE** – Sets the standard block size for the database. The standard block size is used for the SYSTEM tablespace and will be used for other tablespaces by default. Oracle can support up to four additional nonstandard block sizes.
- **COMPATIBLE** – Used to make Oracle act as if it were an earlier release of the software.
- **DIAGNOSTIC_DEST** – Used to determine the location of the Automatic Diagnostic Repository.

- **LOG_ARCHIVE_DEST_n** – Determines where to write Archived Redo Logs.
- **OPEN_CURSORS** – Sets the maximum number of open cursors for an individual session.
- **SESSIONS** – Sets the maximum number of sessions that can connect to the database.

Displaying Database Parameters

You can determine the values of instance parameters in from either SQL*Plus or SQL Developer. Parameter values can be determined by querying the V$PARAMETER view:

```
SELECT name, value
FROM   v$parameter
WHERE  name LIKE '%size%';

NAME                          VALUE
--------------- ------
sga_max_size                  1073741824
shared_pool_size              0
large_pool_size               0
java_pool_size                0
streams_pool_size             0
shared_pool_reserved_size     18454937
java_max_sessionspace_size    0
db_block_size                 8192
```

You can also use the "show parameter" command to display one or more parameters. The parameter name given in the command is treated as a wildcard. Any parameters for which the supplied value is a part of the name will be displayed:

```
show parameter pool_size

NAME                          TYPE        VALUE
----------------------------- ----------- -----
global_context_pool_size      string
java_pool_size                big integer 0
large_pool_size               big integer 0
olap_page_pool_size           big integer 0
shared_pool_size              big integer 0
streams_pool_size             big integer 0
```

If you give a complete parameter name, only the one parameter will be returned:

```
show parameter large_pool_size

NAME                          TYPE        VALUE
----------------------------- ----------- -----
large_pool_size               big integer 0
```

You can use the "show spparameter" command to view parameter values that have been specified in the server parameter file. Since there is nothing in the value column below, the parameter value has not been specified in the file:

```
show spparameter shared_pool_reserved_size

SID NAME                          TYPE        VALUE
--- ----------------------------- ----------- ------
*   shared_pool_reserved_size     big integer
```

The following database views can be used to locate information about database parameters.

- **V$PARAMETER** – Displays the values of initialization parameters in effect for the current session.
- **V$PARAMETER2** – Similar to V$PARAMETER. However it is easier to distinguish list parameter values in this view because each list parameter value appears in a separate row.
- **V$SYSTEM_PARAMETER** – Displays the values of initialization parameters in effect for the instance.
- **V$SPPARAMETER** – Displays the current contents of the SPFILE. It returns FALSE values in the ISSPECIFIED column if an SPFILE is not being used by the instance.

Altering Initialization Parameter Values

There are two broad classes of initialization parameters: static and dynamic. Static parameters affect the entire database and can only be modified by changing the PFILE or SPFILE. They will require a database shutdown before taking effect. Dynamic parameters can be altered while the instance is running and will take effect without requiring a shutdown. Dynamic parameters can be further subdivided into session and system-level parameters:

- **Session-level parameters** – Affect only a single session. These can be altered using the ALTER SESSION command and will only affect the session in which that command is executed. The changed values expire as soon as that session is closed.
- **System-level parameters** – Affect the entire database and all sessions. They can be set with the ALTER SYSTEM command and can either be temporary or permanent.

You can use the ALTER SYSTEM statement with the SET clause to alter initialization parameter values. When doing so, there is a second optional SCOPE clause that determines the scope of the change. For instances that are not using a server parameter file, only the SCOPE=MEMORY is a valid option. Permanent parameter changes will have to be made by manually altering the text-based parameter file.

- **SCOPE = SPFILE** – The change is applied in the server parameter file only. No change is made to the current instance. The change is effective at the next startup and is persistent. This scope can be used with either static or dynamic parameters.
- **SCOPE = MEMORY** – The change is applied in memory only. The change is made to the current instance and is effective immediately. The change is not persistent because the server parameter file is not updated. This scope is only valid for dynamic parameters.
- **SCOPE = BOTH** – The change is applied in both the server parameter file and memory. The change is made to the current instance and is effective immediately. The effect is persistent because the server parameter file is updated. This scope is only valid for dynamic parameters.

There are two more optional modifiers that add additional functionality to the ALTER SYSTEM command:

- **COMMENT** – For instances using a server parameter file, this clause can be used with the SPFILE and BOTH options to add a comment to the SPFILE along with the changed parameter (i.e. 'Changed on 2/28/2014 by Matt Morris').
- **DEFERRED** – This keyword is valid for dynamic parameters with the MEMORY and BOTH options for parameters that are session-specific. The change will be made effective only for future sessions.

Oracle Data Structures

Articulate the various schema objects in a relational database

Objects in the Oracle Database fall into two broad classes, schema objects and non-schema objects. If an object is associated with a particular schema, then it is a schema object. Conversely, if not, it is a non-schema object. A database schema is owned by and has the same name as an Oracle database user. The user and schema are not the same thing. However, since they are created simultaneously, cannot exist independently, and dropping a user drops the schema of the same name – the two are often treated as the same thing. The schema itself is defined as a collection of logical structures of data, or objects. Schema objects are created and manipulated via SQL statements. A partial list of schema objects follows:

- Constraints
- Database triggers
- Indexes
- Sequences
- Synonyms
- Tables
- Views

Nonschema Objects are also stored in the database and can be created and manipulated with SQL. However, they are not contained in a schema and (with the exception of users) have no affinity to any particular schema. A partial list of these includes:

- Directories
- Roles
- Rollback segments
- Tablespaces
- Users

Schemas provide for a way to separate the objects of different users. User A stores their tables in Schema A and User B stores their tables in Schema B. This makes it easier for users to keep track of their information and also provides a level of security. By default, users have access only to objects in their own schemas unless the owning user specifically grants them access. Schemas also allow for resource allocation. The database administrator can grant space in tablespaces to each user's schema based on their job role and requirements.

When DML and DDL statements are executed, Oracle always determines what schema is being affected by the statement. Ideally, you should always explicitly define the schema by prefixing the object name with the schema and a period. This makes the intent of the statement perfectly clear by avoiding ambiguity and also means the Oracle does not have to spend parse time determining which schema should be referenced. In practice, however, schemas are left off more often than they are specified. The following statement works because the table being queried is in the schema of the current session:

```
SELECT emp_first, emp_last, emp_job, salary
FROM   employees
WHERE  emp_job = 'SVP';
ORDER BY 2, 1;

EMP_FIRST  EMP_LAST   EMP_JOB    SALARY
---------- ---------- ---------- ------
Rick       Jameson    SVP        145200
Rob        Stoner     SVP        149100
```

Because it works, SQL developers often do not explicitly define the schema. The following query returns the exact same result as the one above:

```
SELECT emp_first, emp_last, emp_job, salary
FROM   ocpguru.employees
WHERE  emp_job = 'SVP';
ORDER BY 2, 1;

EMP_FIRST  EMP_LAST   EMP_JOB    SALARY
---------- ---------- ---------- ------
Rick       Jameson    SVP        145200
Rob        Stoner     SVP        149100
```

When the object being referenced by a DML statement is not in the current schema, however, normally it is required that the schema where the object exists be added to the statement. It is possible to reference objects in different schema without a schema reference if a synonym has been created to the destination object. An Oracle synonym is simply a database object that redirects SQL references against a defined name to a specific schema object. Some of the most common types of schema objects include:

- **Tables** -- A table is a set of rows organized into columns. A column identifies an attribute of the entity described by the table, whereas a row identifies an instance of the entity.
- **Indexes** -- Indexes are schema objects that contain an entry for each indexed row of the table or table cluster. Indexes provide direct, fast access to rows. The Oracle Database supports several types of index.
- **Partitions** -- Partitions are pieces of large tables and indexes. Each partition has its own name and may optionally have its own storage characteristics.
- **Views** -- Views are customized presentations of data in one or more tables or other views. Views are effectively stored SQL queries and do not actually contain data.
- **Sequences** -- A sequence is a user-created object that can be shared by multiple users to generate integers. Typically, you use sequences to generate primary key values.
- **Synonyms** -- A synonym is an alias for another schema object.
- **PL/SQL subprograms and packages** -- PL/SQL is the Oracle procedural extension of SQL. A PL/SQL subprogram is a named PL/SQL block that can be invoked with a set of parameters.

Perform different index scans and relate them to index types

Indexes are optional structures that can be associated with a table or table cluster, to potentially speed data access and reduce disk I/O. A heap-organized table with no index or materialized view will always require a full table scan when queried. Indexes are logically and physically independent of the data in the objects with which they are associated. Creating or dropping an index can does not physically affect the table it is based on. SQL statements issued against a table do not need to be changed to account for the presence or absence of an index on it. An index can only affect (potentially) the execution speed of a given SQL statement.

Once created, indexes are maintained automatically by Oracle, changing to reflect changes to the table they are based on. It should be noted that while indexes might improve the speed of SELECT operations issued against the table, they always degrade to some degree the speed of DML operations issued against the table because of the requirement to maintain all associated indexes when the table data is changed. Indexes can be unique or nonunique.

- **Unique** -- A unique index constrains data entry to ensure that no two rows of a table have duplicate values in the key column or columns. The data in the leaf blocks of a unique index is sorted only by key.
- **Nonunique** – Nonunique indexes permit duplicate values in the indexed column(s). Nonunique indexes include the rowid in the key in sorted order.

B-Tree Indexes

B-tree indexes are the standard index type for Oracle. B-trees, short for balanced trees, are the choice for primary key and highly-selective indexes. A B-tree index associates a key with a row or range of rows. This provides excellent retrieval performance for a wide range of queries, including exact match and range searches. There are several subtypes of B-Tree indexes:

- **Index-organized tables** -- An index-organized table differs from a heap-organized because the data is itself the index.
- **Reverse key indexes** -- The bytes of the index key are reversed.
- **Descending indexes** -- This type of index stores data on a particular column or columns in descending order.

- **B-tree cluster indexes** -- This type of index is used to index a table cluster key. Instead of pointing to a row, the key points to the block that contains rows related to the cluster key.

Index-Organized Tables

Heap-organized tables store data in no defined order -- essentially putting data where there is an open space. An index-organized table (IOT) stores the rows of data in a B-tree index structure. The rows in an IOT are stored in an index defined on the primary key for the table. Each index entry in the B-tree also stores the non-key column values. IOTs are accessed and maintained using SQL statements in the same fashion as heap-organized tables. They provide fast access to table rows when queried by primary key or a valid prefix of the key. Because rows are stored in primary key order, range access by the primary key or prefix involves minimal block I/Os. IOTs also do not have the space overhead of a separate primary key index. They are most useful when the vast majority of queries against the table use the primary key.

Bitmap Indexes

In a bitmap index, the database stores a bitmap for each index key. Each bit in the bitmap corresponds to a possible rowid. If the bit is set, then the row with the corresponding rowid contains the key value. A mapping function converts the bit position to an actual rowid. Unlike B-tree indexes, where one index entry points to a single row, in a bitmap index, each index key stores pointers to multiple rows. Bitmap indexes are best for environments in which queries reference many columns in an ad hoc fashion. Bitmap indexes work well in the following situations:

- The indexed columns have low cardinality.
- Queries include predicates on multiple bitmap-indexed columns that together result in good selectivity.
- The indexed table is either read-only or not subject to significant modification by DML statements.

If the indexed column in a single row is updated, then the database locks the index key entry and not the individual bit mapped to the updated row. Because a given key may point to many rows, DML on indexed data typically locks all of these rows. For this reason, bitmap indexes are generally not appropriate for applications with concurrent updates such as OLTP systems. Through compression techniques, bitmap indexes can generate a large number of rowids with minimal I/O. Combining bitmap indexes on non-selective columns allows efficient AND and OR operations with a large number of rowids. They are very efficient in queries with COUNT(), because the query can be satisfied by simply combining the appropriate bitmap indexes and counting the number of ones in the resulting bitmap.

Bitmap Join Indexes

As another path to facilitate join operations, you can create a bitmap join index. This is a bitmap index for the join of two or more tables that indexes the rows of one table based on the column values of a joined table. Creating a bitmap join index is a means of reducing the volume of data that must be joined by performing restrictions in advance. For each value in a column of a table, a bitmap join index stores the rowids of corresponding rows in another table. Bitmap join indexes are much more efficient in storage than materialized join views.

Composite Indexes

A composite index contains multiple columns of a table in the key. When creating a composite index, the order of the columns is critical. The most commonly accessed columns should be first. Composite indexes can speed retrieval of data for SELECT statements in which the WHERE clause references all or the leading portion of the columns in the composite index.

The Optimizer may also choose to use a composite index even if the leading column is not in the predicate. It can do this through use of an index skip scan. Scanning index blocks can often be faster than scanning table data blocks. When skip scanning is used, a composite index is split logically into smaller subindexes. The number of logical subindexes is determined by the number of distinct values in the initial column. If the composite index has few distinct values in the leading column but many distinct values in the nonleading key of the index, skip scanning may be useful.

Access Paths

An access path is the way in which data is retrieved from the database. The access path for a full table scan, for example, is different from the access path using the primary key index. The optimizer selects from the available access paths for a given statement and the estimated cost of using each path or combination of paths. Oracle has numerous different access paths that it can select from, including the following:

- **Full table scans** -- Every row from the scanned table is read in chunks of DB_FILE_MULTIBLOCK_READ_COUNT blocks, and any rows that do not meet the selection criteria are filtered out. The database will sequentially scan all data blocks in the segment that are under the high water mark.
- **Rowid scans** –The database obtains the rowids of the selected rows. This can be from the statement WHERE clause or via an index scan. It then uses the data file and data block information from the rowid to locate each selected row.
- **Index scans** -- This scan searches the index corresponding to the indexed column values accessed by the SQL statement. Typically the database retrieves data by alternately reading an index block and then a table block using the rowid from the index. When the SQL statement accesses only columns that are part of the index, then the required column values are pulled directly from the index rather than accessing the table itself.
- **Full Index Scan** -- The database reads the entire index in order one block at a time. A full index scan is available if a predicate in the SQL statement references a column in the index, and in some

circumstances when no predicate is specified. A full scan can eliminate sorting because the data is ordered by index key.

- **Fast Full Index Scan** -- This is a full index scan in which the database accesses the data in the index itself without accessing the table. The database reads the index blocks in no particular order with DB_FILE_MULTIBLOCK_READ_COUNT blocks read at a time. Fast full index scans are an alternative to a full table scan if the index contains all columns needed for the query and no NULL rows can be returned. This may be because the table column has a NOT NULL constraint or the predicate filters out NULL values.
- **Index Range Scan** -- This is an ordered scan of an index to access selective data where 0, 1, or more values are possible for an index key. The selectivity is the percentage of rows in the table that the query selects and is tied to a query predicate, such as WHERE last_name LIKE 'A%'.
- **Index join** -- This access method joins several indexes for a given table that collectively contain all of its columns referenced by the query. When this method is used, no table access is required because the required column values can be retrieved from the joined indexes.
- **Index Unique Scan** -- In contrast to an index range scan, an index unique scan must have either 0 or 1 rowids associated with an index key. A unique scan is used when a predicate references all of the columns in a UNIQUE index key using an equality operator. An index unique scan stops processing as soon as it finds the first record because no second record is possible.
- **Index Skip Scan** -- An index skip scan uses logical subindexes of a composite index. The database will "skip" through a single index as if it were searching separate indexes. Skip scanning is beneficial if there are few distinct values in the leading column of a composite index and many distinct values in the nonleading key of the index. The database can choose to perform an index skip scan when the leading column of the composite index is not specified in a query predicate.
- **Cluster scans** -- This is used to retrieve data from a table stored in an indexed table cluster. All rows with the same cluster key value are stored in the same data block. The database scans the cluster index to obtain the rowid for a selected row and then locates the rows using it.

- **Hash scans** -- This is used to locate rows in a hash cluster. In a hash cluster, all rows with the same hash value are stored in the same data block. The database applies a hash function to a cluster key value specified by the statement and scans all data blocks containing rows with the resulting hash value.

Leverage partitioning in an Oracle database

Partitioning improves Oracle's ability to support very large tables by breaking them into smaller and more manageable pieces called partitions. Partitioned tables facilitate SQL tuning by allowing SQL statements to avoid scanning partitions that can be determined not to hold the required data using partition pruning. Partitioning can also facilitate SQL tuning by breaking down large joins of similarly-partitioned objects by using partition-wise joins. Partitioning of tables and indexes works hand-in-hand with parallel queries to improve performance in data warehouses. When an object in the database is partitioned, it is possible for parallel server processes to scan individual table partitions or index partitions when doing so makes sense.

Partitioning Methods

There are three fundamental methods used to control how data is distributed into partitions: Range, Hash, and List. When partitioning data using these methods, it is possible to partition a table at a single-level, or to partition it at two levels for composite partitioning. There are advantages and design considerations for both methods. The specific needs of a given table determine which strategy is more appropriate.

Single-Level Partitioning

In single-level partitioning, a table is defined by specifying one of the following three methodologies, where one or more columns in the table act as the partitioning key:

- **Range Partitioning** -- This method maps data to partitions based on ranges of values of the partitioning key. Each of the partitions is defined with a range of values that determines which records should be placed in it. This is the most common type of partitioning and is often used with dates. Partitions are created with a VALUES LESS THAN clause, which specifies a non-inclusive upper bound for the partitions. Rows that have partitioning key values equal to or higher than this literal are added to the next higher partition. The lower bound is implied by the VALUES LESS THAN clause of the previous partition. The first partition has no lower bound. The highest partition can use a MAXVALUE literal. This represents a virtual infinite value that sorts higher than any other possible value for the partitioning key, including NULL.
- **Hash Partitioning** -- This method uses a hashing algorithm to map data to partitions using the partitioning key that you identify. The hashing algorithm is designed to evenly distribute rows among each of the partitions. This is an ideal method to distribute data evenly across devices. It is easier to implement than range partitioning. Hash partitioning is especially useful when the data to be partitioned is not historical or has no obvious partitioning key.
- **List Partitioning** -- This method allows you to specify a list of discrete values for the partitioning key in the description for each partition. In this fashion, you can control exactly how rows map to partitions. List partitioning provides the ability to group unordered and unrelated sets of data. In list partitioning, the DEFAULT partition provides a partition to store all values that are not explicitly mapped to any other partition.

Composite Partitioning

This strategy combines the basic data distribution methods. In composite partitioning, a table is partitioned by one data distribution method and then each partition is further subdivided into subpartitions using a second data distribution method. It is possible for the partitioning methods at the two levels to be the same, or different. Composite partitioning provides higher degrees of potential partition pruning and finer granularity of data placement. The possible composite partitioning methods are:

- Range-Range Partitioning
- Range-Hash Partitioning
- Range-List Partitioning
- List-Range Partitioning
- List-Hash Partitioning
- List-List Partitioning

Partition Pruning

One of the largest factors to improve SQL performance that partitioning provides is partition pruning (also known as partition elimination). Partition pruning has the potential to improve query performance by multiple orders of magnitude. When tables are partitioned by keys that are used as conditions in queries, Oracle may be able to eliminate the vast majority of partitions from consideration before ever starting to retrieve data. Partition pruning works with all of Oracle's other performance features. Partition pruning can be used with any indexing technique, join technique, or parallel access method.

Not all predicates can be used for partition pruning. The relevant predicates than can be used with each partition type are:

- **Range** – Pruning can occur with range, LIKE, equality or IN-list predicates.
- **List** – Pruning can occur with range, LIKE, equality or IN-list predicates.
- **Hash** – Pruning can occur with equality or IN-list predicates.

Partition-Wise Joins

The performance of multi-table joins can be dramatically improved by using partition-wise joins. Partition-wise joins are possible when two tables that are partitioned on the join key are being joined. They can also occur when a reference partitioned table is joined with its parent. When partition-wise joins are performed, Oracle breaks a large join into smaller joins that occur between each of the partitions. This allows the overall join to be completed in less time and offers substantial performance benefits for serial and parallel execution.

Partitioned Indexes

Indexes can either be partitioned independently of the table they are based on (global indexes) or linked to the base table's partitioning method (local indexes). As a general rule, global indexes are used for OLTP applications and local indexes for data warehousing or DSS applications. Global indexes are often used for highly selective keys that do not include the partition key.

Each partition of a local index is associated with exactly one partition of the table. Oracle keeps the index partitions synchronized with the table partitions, and makes each table-index pair independent. If one partition's data becomes invalid or unavailable, only the single partition is affected. It is not possible to explicitly add a partition to a local index. New partitions are added to local indexes when a partition is added to the underlying table. Likewise, local index partitions are dropped only when a partition from the underlying table is dropped.

Use the data dictionary and the dynamic performance views

A critical aspect of the Oracle database is its data dictionary. The data dictionary is a read-only set of tables that provides metadata about the database. Among other things, the Oracle data dictionary contains the following:

- Definitions of every schema object in the database, including default values for columns and integrity constraint information
- The amount of space allocated for and currently used by the schema objects

- The names of Oracle Database users, privileges and roles granted to users, and auditing information related to users

The dictionary is central to managing data and objects for every Oracle database. Oracle must access the data dictionary to find information about users, schema objects, and storage structures. The data dictionary is modified every time that a DDL statement is issued in the database.

The data dictionary data is stored inside database tables, just like user data. Because of this, it is possible to query the data using SQL. You can use SELECT statements to locate tables in a schema, determine their structure and any privileges you have on them, see what other objects in the database reference them, and so forth.

The data dictionary consists of two types of objects: base tables and views.

- **Base tables** – The underlying tables of the data dictionary store information about the database. Only Oracle Database should write to and read from these tables through the use of DDL commands. There is very seldom a need for users to access the base tables directly. The information in these tables is normalized and most data is stored in a cryptic format with equally cryptic table names.
- **Views** – Data dictionary views are designed to decode the base table data into useful information using joins and WHERE clauses to simplify the information. Some views are accessible to all database users, and others are intended only for administrators.

The majority of the Oracle data dictionary views are grouped into three sets: DBA, ALL, and USER. By querying the appropriate views, you can access the relevant information. Not all data dictionary view sets will have all three members. For example, the data dictionary contains a DBA_LOCK view but no ALL_LOCK view.

- **DBA_** – These views show data dictionary objects across all schemas. The views are intended to be used by people with Database Administrator-level privileges.
- **ALL_** – These views show data dictionary objects across multiple schemas. The objects shown are filtered based on object level privileges, however. Objects in schemas other than the user querying the view will only be shown if the user has privileges on the object in the other schema. Because the ALL_ views obey the current set of enabled roles, query results will depend on which roles are enabled.
- **USER_** – These views show only data dictionary objects that exist in the schema that is performing the query. The USER views lack the OWNER column that exists in the DBA_ and ALL_ views, since the information is redundant.

The DICTIONARY view contains the names and abbreviated descriptions of all data dictionary views. The following query of this view includes partial sample output:

```
SELECT *
FROM   dictionary
WHERE  table_name LIKE '%ALL_TABLES'
ORDER BY table_name;

TABLE_NAME       COMMENTS
---------------- ------------------------
ALL_ALL_TABLES   Description of all object and relational
                   tables accessible to the user
ALL_TABLES       Description of relational tables accessible
                   to the user
DBA_ALL_TABLES   Description of all object and relational
                   tables in the database
USER_ALL_TABLES  Description of all object and relational
                   tables owned by the users
```

Dynamic Performance Views

Oracle contains a set of views maintained by the database server called dynamic performance views. The data in these views is continuously updated while a database is in use, and relates primarily to performance. The views act as if they are based on regular database tables, but this is not the case. The views provide data on internal disk structures and memory structures. It's possible to select from these views, but not update or alter them. After installation, only the SYS user or a user with the SYSDBA role can access the dynamic performance views. Only simple queries are supported against the views. Because the information in the V$ views is dynamic, read consistency is not guaranteed when a SELECT is issued against them:

- **V$ Views** – Dynamic performance views are identified by the prefix V_$. However, each has a public synonym using the same name but with the prefix V$. All users should access only the V$ objects, not the V_$ objects. For an instance that is not mounted, only the V$ views that read from memory are accessible. V$ views that read data from disk require that the database be mounted. Some of the V$ views require that the database be open.
- **GV$ Views** – For most V$ views, Oracle has a corresponding GV$ (global V$) view. GV$ views are for use in databases making use of Real Application Clusters. Querying a GV$ view retrieves the V$ view information from all available instances of the database. GV$ views contain an extra column named INST_ID that displays the instance number from which the associated V$ view information was obtained.

Identify the various tools for data movement and analysis

SQL*Loader

The SQL*Loader utility allows you to load data from external flat files into Oracle database tables. The parsing engine of SQL*Loader is very versatile and puts few limitations on the format of the data in the external file. SQL*Loader recognizes the data in the data file as records whether it is in fixed record format, variable record format, or stream record format. The record format is normally specified in the control file using the INFILE parameter. If no record format is specified, then the default is stream record format. SQL*Loader can perform the following tasks:

- Load data from multiple data files in a single load session.
- Load data into multiple tables in a single load session.
- Load data from different character sets.
- Load only selected data from a file.
- Load data across a network.
- Use SQL functions to transform the data before loading it.
- Generate unique sequential key values while loading.
- Use the operating system's file system to access the data files.
- Load data from disk, tape, or named pipe.
- Generate error reports to aid troubleshooting.
- Load complex object-relational data.
- Use secondary data files for loading LOBs and collections.

SQL*Loader sessions make use of the following files:

- **Control** – Defines the format of the data file and controls the behavior of SQL*Loader.
- **Data** – One or more data files will contain the information to be loaded.
- **Log** – Contains a log of the actions performed by SQL*Loader and errors encountered.
- **Bad** – Contains all records that could not be loaded due to errors.
- **Discard** – Contains all records that the control file identified to be bypassed.

The sqlldr executable is used to invoke SQL*Loader. It is optionally followed by parameters that establish session characteristics. Parameters can also be specified using the following methods instead of the command line:

- Parameters can be added to a parameter file. To use a parameter file, the name of the file can be supplied in the command line using the PARFILE parameter.
- Some parameters can be specified within the SQL*Loader control file using the OPTIONS clause.

If the same parameter is specified on the command line and in a parameter file or OPTIONS clause, the value in the command line is used.

The SQL*Loader control file is a text file that tells SQL*Loader where to find the data file, the format to use in parsing the data, what table(s) to insert the data in to, and more. A control file has three loosely-defined sections:

- The first section contains session-wide information such as global options, the input data file location, and the data to be loaded.
- The second section consists of one or more INTO TABLE blocks. The blocks hold information about the destination table.
- The third section is optional and, if present, contains input data.

SQL*Loader has two methods of inserting data into Oracle tables, Conventional Path and Direct Load options. In conventional path, SQL*Loader effectively creates INSERT statements for the records in the file to be loaded and passes them to the Oracle SQL Parser to be handled. When using Direct Path, SQL*Loader bypasses SQL and the parser and loads data directly into the target table(s). Direct Path load is much faster, but Conventional Path is more flexible. Some restrictions of the Direct Path load are:

- It cannot run concurrently with other transactions against the target table.
- Triggers on the table do not fire.
- Data is written above the high-water mark of the table even if there is space below.
- Clustered tables are not supported.
- Foreign Key constraints are disabled during the load.

External Tables

External tables are defined as tables that do not reside in the database. It's possible to have tables in any format for which an access driver is provided. Inside the Oracle data dictionary is stored metadata describing an external table. With this metadata, Oracle provides SQL access to the external table as if it were a regular database table. It's possible to perform SELECT and JOIN operations, or create views or synonyms against external tables. It is not possible to perform DML operations or create indexes on external tables.

The metadata for external tables is created using the ORGANIZATION EXTERNAL clause of the CREATE TABLE statement. An external table definition acts as a view against the external data. An access driver is mechanism by which the external data is read. Oracle Database provides two access drivers for external tables: ORACLE_LOADER and ORACLE_DATAPUMP. ORACLE_LOADER reads data from external files using the Oracle Loader technology using a subset of the control file syntax of the SQL*Loader utility. ORACLE_DATAPUMP allows you to read data from the database and insert it into an external table, and then reload it into an Oracle Database. Note that while ORACLE_DATAPUMP allows writing to external files, the functionality is not performed via DML statements.

The ANALYZE statement is not supported for gathering statistics for external tables, but you can use the DBMS_STATS package. Virtual columns are not supported on external tables. For an external table, the DROP TABLE statement removes only metadata in the database. It has no effect on the actual data outside of the database.

You create external tables using the CREATE TABLE statement with an ORGANIZATION EXTERNAL clause. This statement creates only metadata in the data dictionary. The following example creates an external table using the ORACLE_LOADER access method.

```
CREATE TABLE phone_list_ext (
  employee_id         VARCHAR2(5),
  first_name          VARCHAR2(50),
  last_name           VARCHAR2(50),
  phone               VARCHAR2(20)
)
ORGANIZATION EXTERNAL (
  TYPE ORACLE_LOADER
  DEFAULT DIRECTORY ext_tables
  ACCESS PARAMETERS (
    RECORDS DELIMITED BY NEWLINE
    FIELDS TERMINATED BY ','
    MISSING FIELD VALUES ARE NULL
    (
      employee_id         CHAR(5),
      first_name          CHAR(50),
      last_name           CHAR(50),
      phone               CHAR(20)
    )
  )
  LOCATION ('phone_list.txt')
)
PARALLEL 2
REJECT LIMIT UNLIMITED;
```

The example above uses the ORACLE_LOADER access driver. This driver is used for reading text files. Essentially any file that SQL*Loader can read from can be used as an external table. The parameters in the ACCESS PARAMETERS clause are opaque to the database. These parameters are specific to the access driver. Oracle provides these parameters to the access driver when the external table is accessed. The PARALLEL clause enables parallel query on the data sources. The REJECT LIMIT clause specifies that there is no limit on the number of errors that can occur during a query of the external data.

Only the following ALTER TABLE Clause options are allowed on external tables:

- **REJECT LIMIT** – Changes the reject limit.
- **PROJECT COLUMN REFERENCED** – The access driver processes only the columns in the select list of the query. This setting may not provide a consistent set of rows when querying a different column list from the same external table but can speed up access.

- **PROJECT COLUMN ALL** – The access driver processes all of the columns defined on the external table. This setting always provides a consistent set of rows when querying an external table. This is the default.
- **DEFAULT DIRECTORY** – Changes the default directory specification.

Oracle Data Pump

Oracle Data Pump is designed to provide high-speed movement of data and metadata from one database to another. It replaces the export/import functionality that existed in earlier releases of Oracle. Data Pump is made up of three distinct parts:

- **expdp and impdp** – These are command-line clients that use the procedures provided in the DBMS_DATAPUMP package to execute export and import commands. They accept parameters entered at the command line that enable the exporting and importing of data and metadata for a complete database or for subsets of a database.
- **DBMS_DATAPUMP** – Also known as the Data Pump API, this package provides a high-speed mechanism to move all or part of the data and metadata for a site from one database to another. DBMS_DATAPUMP can be used independently of the impdp and expdp clients.
- **DBMS_METADATA** – Also known as the Metadata API, this package provides a centralized facility for the extraction, manipulation, and re-creation of dictionary metadata. DBMS_METADATA can be used independently of the impdp and expdp clients.

Data Pump jobs use a master table, a master process, and worker processes to perform the work and keep track of progress:

- **Master Table** – A master table is used to track the progress within a job while the data and metadata are being transferred. It is implemented as a user table within the database. A user performing an impdp or expdp must have the CREATE TABLE system privilege for the master table to be created plus sufficient tablespace quota. The master table will have the same name as the job that created it. A Data Pump job cannot have the same name as an existing table or view in that schema. The information in the master table is used to restart a job.
- **Master process** – A master process is created for every Data Pump Export job and Data Pump Import job. It controls the entire job, including communicating with the clients, creating and controlling a pool of worker processes, and performing logging operations.
- **Worker Process** – The master process allocates work to be executed to worker processes that perform the data and metadata processing within an operation. Data Pump can employ multiple worker processes, running in parallel, to increase job performance.

There are different expdp modes for unloading different portions of the database. The mode is specified using the appropriate parameter. The available modes are:

- **Full** – In a full database export, the entire database is unloaded. This mode requires the user performing the export to have the DATAPUMP_EXP_FULL_DATABASE role. Specified using the FULL parameter.
- **Schema** – This is the default export mode. If you have the DATAPUMP_EXP_FULL_DATABASE role, then you can provide a list of schemas to export. Otherwise you can export only your own schema. Specified using the SCHEMAS parameter.
- **Table** – In table mode, only a specified set of tables, partitions, and their dependent objects are unloaded. You must have the DATAPUMP_EXP_FULL_DATABASE role to export tables that are not in your own schema. Specified using the TABLES parameter.
- **Tablespace** – In tablespace mode, only the tables contained in a specified set of tablespaces are unloaded. If a table is unloaded, then its dependent objects are also unloaded. Privileged users get

all tables. Unprivileged users get only the tables in their own schemas. Specified using the TABLESPACES parameter.

- **Transportable Tablespace** – In transportable tablespace mode, only the metadata for the tables (and their dependent objects) within a specified set of tablespaces is exported. The tablespace data files are copied in a separate operation. Specified using the TRANSPORT_TABLESPACES parameter.

expdp Parameters

The following parameters are applicable to expdp:

- **ATTACH** – Attaches the client session to an existing export job and automatically places you in the interactive-command interface.
- **CONTENT** – Enables you to filter what Export unloads: data only, metadata only, or both.
- **DIRECTORY** – Specifies the default location to which Export can write the dump file set and the log file.
- **DUMPFILE** – Specifies the names, and optionally, the directory objects of dump files for an export job.
- **ESTIMATE** – Specifies the method that Export will use to estimate how much disk space each table in the export job will consume (in bytes).
- **ESTIMATE_ONLY** – Instructs Export to estimate the space that a job would consume, without actually performing the export operation.
- **EXCLUDE** – Enables you to filter the metadata that is exported by specifying objects and object types to be excluded from the export operation.
- **FILESIZE** – Specifies the maximum size of each dump file.
- **FULL** – Specifies that you want to perform a full database mode export.
- **INCLUDE** – Enables you to filter the metadata that is exported by specifying objects and object types for the current export mode.
- **JOB_NAME** – Used to identify the export job in subsequent actions.
- **LOGFILE** – Specifies the name, and optionally, a directory, for the log file of the export job.
- **PARFILE** – Specifies the name of an export parameter file.

- **QUERY** – Allows you to specify a query clause that is used to filter the data that gets exported.
- **SCHEMAS** – Specifies that you want to perform a schema-mode export.
- **TABLES** – Specifies that you want to perform a table-mode export.
- **TABLESPACES** – Specifies a list of tablespace names to be exported in tablespace mode.

impdp Parameters

Many of the above parameters are also applicable to impdp. In addition, several of the more common impdp parameters are:

- **REUSE_DATAFILES** – Specifies whether the import job should reuse existing data files for tablespace creation.
- **SQLFILE** – Specifies a file into which all of the SQL DDL that Import would have executed, based on other parameters, is written.
- **STATUS** – Specifies the frequency at which the job status display is updated.
- **TABLE_EXISTS_ACTION** – Tells import what to do if the table it is trying to create already exists.
- **REMAP_DATAFILE** – Changes the name of the source data file to the target data file name in all SQL statements where the source data file is referenced.
- **REMAP_SCHEMA** – Loads all objects from the source schema into a target schema.
- **REMAP_TABLE** – Allows you to rename tables during an import operation.
- **REMAP_TABLESPACE** – Remaps all objects selected for import with persistent data in the source tablespace to be created in the target tablespace.

Oracle LogMiner

This application allows you to query redo log files through a SQL interface. Oracle LogMiner is accessible through a command-line interface or through the Oracle LogMiner Viewer GUI in Enterprise Manager. Some of the potential uses for data contained in redo log files include:

- Pinpointing when a logical corruption to a database may have begun
- Detecting user error
- Determining what actions you would have to take to perform fine-grained recovery at the transaction level
- Using trend analysis to determine which tables get the most updates and inserts
- Analyzing system behavior and auditing database use through the LogMiner comprehensive relational interface to redo log files

ADRCI

The Automatic Diagnostic Repository Command Interpreter (ADRCI) is a command-line utility that is part of the Oracle fault diagnosability infrastructure. ADRCI's primary functions include:

- Viewing diagnostic data in the Automatic Diagnostic Repository.
- Viewing Health Monitor reports.
- Packaging incident and problem information for Oracle Support.

Diagnostic data viewable from within ADRCI includes incident and problem descriptions, trace files, dumps, health monitor reports, alert log entries, and more. ADRCI can be used in interactive mode or within scripts. ADRCI can also execute scripts of ADRCI commands just as SQL*Plus can execute scripts of SQL and PL/SQL commands. There is no login to ADRCI -- it is secured by OS-level file permissions only.

You can use ADRCI to view the names of trace files that are currently in the ADR. You can view the names of all trace files, or a filtered subset of names. ADRCI has commands to obtain a list of trace files whose file name matches a search string, exist in a particular directory, pertain to a particular incident, or a combination of these. The SHOW TRACEFILE command displays a list of the files in the trace directory and in all incident directories under the current ADR home.

Oracle Database Instance Architecture

Define the main components of an Oracle Instance

The Oracle Relational Database Management System (RDBMS) is an immensely capable (and complex) application designed to provide a comprehensive, open, and integrated information management system. It can manage huge amounts of data in a multiuser environment to provide concurrent access to data for thousands of simultaneous users. It provides a high level of data security, excellent performance, and has extremely effective failure recovery capabilities.

Database vs. Instance

At the highest level, an Oracle database server consists of two distinct components: a database and one or more database instances. In general usage, the term Oracle database is often used to refer to both. The definitions of the two are:

- **Database** – A database is a set of files, located on disk, that store data. These files can exist independently of a database instance.
- **Database instance** – An instance is a set of memory structures that manage database files. An Oracle instance consists of a shared memory area and a set of background processes. An instance can exist independently of database files.

In the conventional configuration, there is a single instance and a single database. However, when using a multi-node Real Application Cluster configuration, there are multiple instances pointing at a single database. The RAC configuration allows for improved scalability, performance, and fault tolerance.

The illustration below shows the primary components of an Oracle instance. There is a view on the Oracle Learning Library that breaks the instance components out to a much more granular level and also shows the database elements as well:

(http://www.oracle.com/webfolder/technetwork/tutorials/obe/db/12c/r1/poster/OUTPUT_poster/poster.html). You do not have to memorize either diagram, but they help you to visualize how the various aspects of the Oracle instance fit together.

Figure 1: Oracle instance components

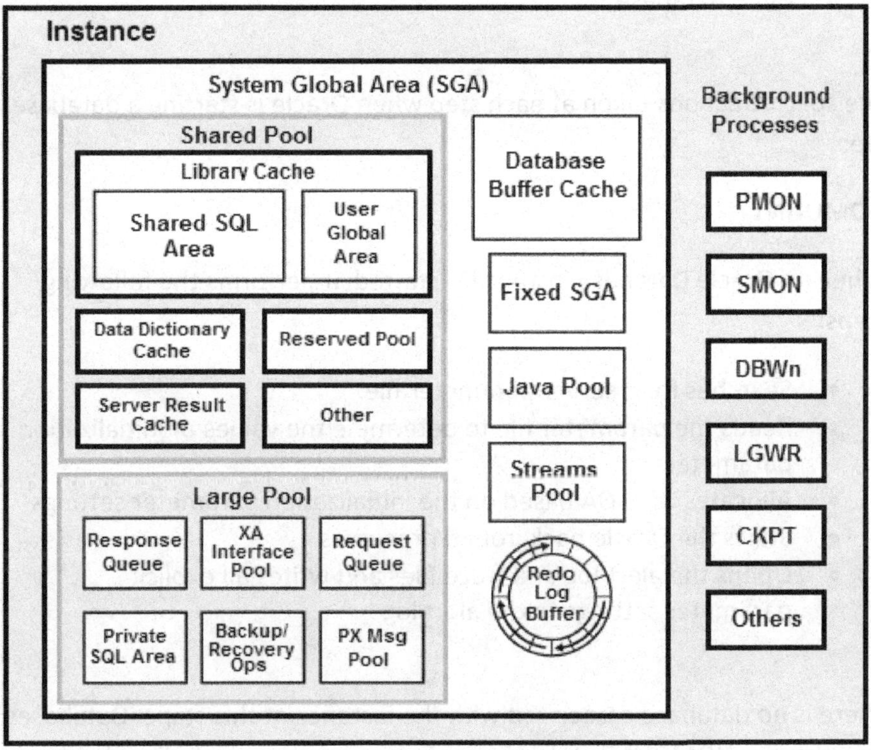

Describe the various stages of a database instance

An Oracle database instance has four distinct phases that it can be in. A complete startup operation for a database that is initially shutdown goes through three steps. Likewise, a complete shutdown or a fully started

Oracle database takes three steps before it is shut down completely. The four phases are:

- **Shut down** -- There are no Oracle processes in memory.
- **Nomount** -- An instance of Oracle is in memory, but it is not yet associated with a database.
- **Mounted** -- An instance of Oracle is started and is associated with a closed database.
- **Open** -- An instance of Oracle is started and is associated with an open database.

The specific actions taken at each step when Oracle is starting a database are:

NOMOUNT

When an Oracle Database instance is started, it performs the following steps:

- Searches for a server parameter file.
- Reads the parameter file to determine the values of initialization parameters
- Allocates the SGA based on the initialization parameter settings
- Starts the Oracle background processes
- Opens the alert log and trace files and writes all explicit parameter settings to the alert log

There is no database associated with the instance at this stage. Databases must be in a NOMOUNT status for various operations, including database creation and certain backup and recovery operations.

MOUNT

When an Oracle database is mounted, Oracle Database performs the following actions:

- It will obtain the names of the database control files via the CONTROL_FILES parameter in the server parameter file.
- The database will open and read control files in order to locate the names of the data files and the online redo log files that it will use when opening the database.

When the database is mounted, it is closed and accessible only to database administrators. There are a number of specific maintenance tasks that can be performed by administrators while the database is closed. However, the database is not available for normal operations.

OPEN

When you open the database, Oracle Database performs the following actions:

- Opens the online data files in tablespaces other than undo tablespaces
- Acquires an undo tablespace
- Opens the online redo log files

Once a mounted database has been opened, it becomes available for normal database operation. Unless it was opened in restricted mode, any valid user can connect to an open database and access its information. The database opens in read/write mode by default. In this mode, users can make changes to the data, generating redo in the online redo log. The database can also be opened in read-only mode. Read-only mode restricts database access to read-only transactions, which cannot write to data files or to online redo log files. However, the database can perform recovery or operations that change the database state without generating redo.

The Oracle Database will automatically perform the following steps whenever an open database is shut down consistently:

CLOSED

When an Oracle database is issued a shutdown command, the database close operation is implicit. The actions taken during the close operation depend on whether the database shutdown is normal or abnormal.

- **Normal Shutdown** -- When a database is closed as part of a SHUTDOWN with any option other than ABORT, the database will write data in the SGA to the data files and online redo log files. The database will then close all online data files and online redo log files. At this point, the database is closed and inaccessible for normal operations. The control files remain open after a database is closed.

- **Abnormal Shutdown** -- When a SHUTDOWN ABORT or an abnormal termination occurs (i.e. a media failure), the instance of an open database closes and the database is shut down instantaneously. The data in the buffers of the SGA is not written out to the data files and redo log files. The database will require instance recovery when the database is next opened. The Oracle Database automatically performs instance recovery when required.

UNMOUNTED

Once the database has been closed, it is unmounted to disassociate it from the instance. Once the database has been unmounted, the control files of the database are closed. The instance remains in memory at this point.

SHUT DOWN

When the database instance shuts down, the SGA ceases to occupy memory, and the Oracle background processes terminate.

When issuing a startup from SQL*Plus, there are several options to determine the state and availability of the database:

- **STARTUP NOMOUNT** – Start the instance without mounting a database. This does not allow access to the database and usually would be done only for database creation or the re-creation of control files.
- **STARTUP MOUNT** – Start the instance and mount the database, but leave it closed. This state allows for certain DBA activities, but does not allow general access to the database.
- **STARTUP OPEN** – Start the instance, and mount and open the database in unrestricted mode, allowing access to all users. This is the default method for starting a database.
- **STARTUP RESTRICT** – Start the instance, and mount and open the database in restricted mode, allowing access for database administrators only.
- **STARTUP FORCE** – Force the instance to start after a startup or shutdown problem by issuing a SHUTDOWN ABORT and then a STARTUP NORMAL.
- **STARTUP OPEN RECOVER** – Start the instance and have complete media recovery begin immediately.

An Oracle instance can be shut down using SQL*Plus by connecting as SYSOPER or SYSDBA and issuing the SHUTDOWN command. For databases managed by Oracle Restart, the srvctl stop database command is the only recommended way to shut down the database. When shutting down a database, there are several different modes to choose from: normal, immediate, transactional, and abort. The difference in the modes is that each waits for certain events to occur before executing the shutdown. There is a one-hour timeout period for these events.

Shutdown Normal

The SQL*Plus SHUTDOWN has a NORMAL clause, but this is optional because normal is the default shutdown method. After a normal shutdown, the database will not require any instance recovery procedure on the next startups. Normal database shutdown proceeds as follows:

- No new connections are allowed after the shutdown is issued.
- The database waits for all currently connected users to disconnect from the database before shutting down.

Shutdown Immediate

To shutdown a database in the immediate mode, issue SHUTDOWN IMMEDIATE from SQL*Plus while connected with the SYSDBA or SYSOPER privilege. The immediate database shutdown is used when the database must be taken down while unattended, or if there is an urgent need to have it down in a short timeframe. After a normal shutdown, the database will not require any instance recovery procedure on the next startup. Immediate database shutdown proceeds as follows:

- Neither new connections, nor new transactions are allowed after the statement is issued.
- Uncommitted transactions are rolled back. If there are long running transactions underway, this method of shutdown might not complete quickly.
- Users currently connected without running transactions are disconnected after rolling back any completed (but uncommitted) transactions.

Shutdown Transactional

To shutdown a database in the transactional mode, issue SHUTDOWN TRANSACTIONAL from SQL*Plus while connected with the SYSDBA or SYSOPER privilege. This mode allows you to perform a planned shutdown of an instance while allowing active transactions to complete first. Shutdown Transaction MAY take longer than a shutdown immediate because transactions in progress at the time the shutdown is initiated don't just have to finish running, but must be committed (or rolled back) as well. It could conceivably be shorter, however. If a million-row update is in process when a SHUTDOWN IMMEDIATE is issued, the DML must run to completion, but will then be rolled back automatically. The same statement with SHUTDOWN transactional must complete, but if committed at completion will end the transaction and allow the database to shutdown. A commit is much faster than a rollback. The next startup of the database will not require any instance recovery procedures. A transactional shutdown prevents clients from losing work. A transactional database shutdown proceeds as follows

- Neither new connections, nor new transactions are allowed after the statement is issued.
- Once all transactions have completed, client sessions to the instance are disconnected.
- After all client sessions are disconnected, the instance shuts down.

Shutdown Abort

To shutdown a database in the abort mode, issue SHUTDOWN ABORT from SQL*Plus while connected with the SYSDBA or SYSOPER privilege. Issuing a shutdown abort will shut down a database instance nearly instantaneously. Shutdown aborts should be avoided if at all possible. You should perform this type of shutdown only when there is a need to shut down the database immediately, or the database is behaving erratically and the other shutdown methods are not working. The next startup of the database will require automatic instance recovery procedures. An aborted database shutdown proceeds as follows:

- Neither new connections, nor new transactions are allowed after the statement is issued.
- Current client SQL statements being processed by Oracle are immediately terminated.
- Uncommitted transactions are not rolled back.
- Oracle implicitly disconnects all connected users.

The actions performed for each of the shutdown options is summarized in the table below:

Shutdown Option	N	T	I	A
New connections allowed	No	No	No	No
Wait for users to log out	Yes	No	No	No
Wait for ongoing transactions to end	Yes	Yes	No	No
Create a checkpoint and close files	Yes	Yes	Yes	No

Figure 2: Database shutdown actions

Shutdown Timeout

All of the shutdown modes that wait for users to disconnect or for transactions to complete only wait for a limited amount of time. If the events blocking the shutdown have not completed within one hour, the shutdown operation will abort with an ORA-01013 error. You'll get the same error if you attempt to abort a shutdown operation manually by hitting Ctrl-C (Oracle recommends against this). After an ORA-01013 occurs, the instance is in an unpredictable state and you should resubmit the SHUTDOWN command. If subsequent SHUTDOWN commands fail, you must issue a SHUTDOWN ABORT. You can then restart the instance.

Articulate the various basic memory structures

When an Oracle instance is started, background processes are initiated and a memory area is allocated in the operating system. This memory area stores numerous different pieces of information required to run the database. Some of the basic memory structures are:

- **System Global Area (SGA)** – The SGA is a group of shared memory structures that contain data and control information for a single Oracle Database instance. The SGA is shared by all server and background processes. Examples of data stored in the SGA include cached data blocks and shared SQL areas.

- **Program global area (PGA)** – A PGA is a memory region that is not shared. It contains data and control information exclusively for the use of an Oracle process. A PGA is created when an Oracle process is started. One PGA exists for each server process and background process. The collection of individual PGAs is the total instance PGA, or instance PGA.
- **User Global Area (UGA)** – The UGA is memory associated with a user session. When using a dedicated server connection, the UGA is stored in the PGA. When using a shared server connection, the UGA is stored in the SGA so that any shared server process has access to it.
- **Software code areas** – Software code areas are portions of memory used to store code that is being run or can be run.

System Global Area

The SGA is the memory container for all of the data required for the database instance. It consists of numerous memory components. Each component is a pool of memory used to satisfy a particular type of memory allocation request. All except the redo log buffer allocate and deallocate space in units of contiguous memory called granules. You can query the V$SGASTAT view for information about SGA components.

The most important elements of the SGA are:

- **Database Buffer Cache** – The database buffer cache stores copies of data blocks read from data files. A buffer is an address where the buffer manager temporarily caches a currently or recently used data block. All users connected to a database instance share access to the buffer cache. The buffer cache is designed to optimize physical I/O; to keep frequently accessed blocks in the buffer cache; and to write infrequently accessed blocks to disk. It makes use of a Least Recently Used (LRU) algorithm to determine what information should be kept in the buffer cache.
- **Redo Log Buffer** – The redo log buffer is a circular buffer that stores redo entries describing changes made to the database. These entries contain the information required to reconstruct changes made to the database by DML or DDL operations.

Database recovery applies redo entries to data files to reconstruct lost changes. The redo entries take up continuous, sequential space in the buffer. The background process log writer (LGWR) writes the redo log buffer to the active online redo log group on disk.

- **Shared Pool** – The shared pool caches various types of program data required by the server. A partial list includes storing parsed SQL, PL/SQL code, system parameters, and data dictionary information. It is involved in almost every operation that occurs in the database. Among other things, every SQL statement issued by users requires an access of the shared pool.
- **Large Pool** – The large pool is an optional memory area in the SGA. It is intended for memory allocations that are larger than is appropriate to store in the shared pool. Examples of this are the UGA for the shared server and the Oracle XA interface and buffers for Recovery Manager (RMAN) I/O slaves.
- **Java Pool** – The Java pool stores all session-specific Java code and data within the Java Virtual Machine (JVM). This includes Java objects that are migrated to the Java session space at end-of-call.
- **Streams Pool** – The Streams pool is used exclusively by Oracle Streams. It stores buffered queue messages and provides memory for Streams capture and apply processes. Unless configured otherwise, the size of the Streams pool starts at zero and grows dynamically as required by Oracle Streams.
- **Fixed SGA** – The fixed SGA is an internal housekeeping area. Among other things, it contains general information required by the background processes about the state of the database and the instance. The size of the fixed SGA is set by the Oracle Database and cannot be altered manually.

Describe how a block of data is written to the database

A data block is the smallest unit of data used by the Oracle Database. At the operating system level, data is stored in bytes and every operating system has a block size. The database issues data requests data in multiples of Oracle Database data blocks which are not synonymous with operating system blocks. The standard block size for a given database is specified by the DB_BLOCK_SIZE initialization parameter. It is possible to specify up to five nonstandard block sizes in addition to the standard size. When specifying a data block size, they should be a multiple of the operating system's block size in order to avoid unnecessary disk I/O.

The data block format used by Oracle is similar whether the data block contains table, index, or clustered data. The below diagram illustrates the format of an Oracle data block.

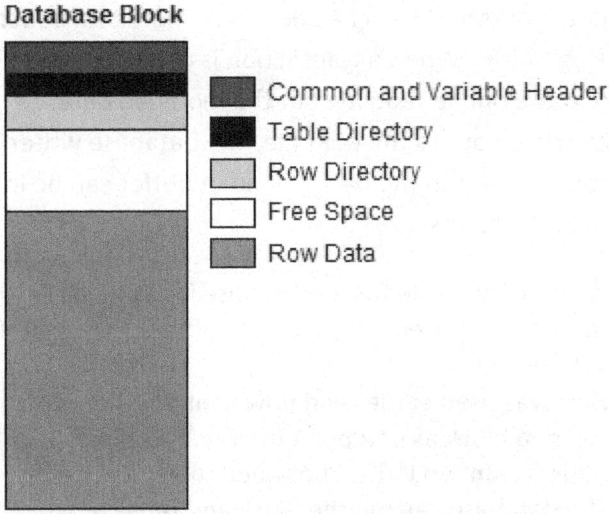

The various elements of an Oracle data block are:

- **Header (Common and Variable)** -- The header contains general block information, such as the block address and the type of segment (for example, data or index).
- **Table Directory** -- This portion of the data block contains information about the table having rows in this block.
- **Row Directory** -- This portion of the data block contains information about the actual rows in the block. This information includes addresses for each row piece in the row data area.
- **Row Data** -- This portion of the data block contains table or index data. Rows can span multiple blocks.
- **Free Space** -- Free space is allocated for insertion of new rows and for updates to rows that require additional space.

Database Buffer Cache

The database buffer cache is the memory area in Oracle that stores the information from data blocks read from data files. Each buffer is a main memory address in which the buffer manager temporarily caches a currently or recently used data block. Access to the database buffer cache is shared by all users concurrently connected to a database instance. The cache is designed to optimize physical I/O operations for the database for both reads and writes to the data. When blocks are written to, the database updates the data blocks in the cache and stores metadata about the changes in the redo log buffer. When a transaction is committed, the redo buffers are written to the online redo log but the modified data block is not immediately written out to the data file. The database writer process (DBW) performs lazy writes in the background. A buffer can be in any of three mutually exclusive states:

- **Unused** -- The buffer is available for use because it has never been used or is currently unused. This type of buffer is the easiest for the database to use.
- **Clean** -- This buffer was used earlier and now contains a read-consistent version of a block as of a point in time. The block contains data but is "clean" so it does not need to be checkpointed. The database can pin the block and reuse it.
- **Dirty** -- The buffer contain modified data that has not yet been written to disk. The database must checkpoint the block before reusing it.

DBW periodically writes cold, dirty buffers to disk. The process will write buffers in the following circumstances:

- A server process cannot find clean buffers for reading new blocks into the database buffer cache.
- If the number of free buffers drops below an internal threshold, and clean buffers are required, then server processes signal DBW to write.

The database buffer cache has a Least Recently Used (LRU) algorithm that tracks buffer usage. The database uses this algorithm to determine which dirty buffers to write out to disk. When dirty buffers reach the cold end of the LRU, they are moved to a write queue. DBW will write the queued buffers to disk, using multiblock writes if possible. When DBW writes buffers to disk, the database must advance the checkpoint. The database checkpoint is the position in the redo thread from which instance recovery must begin.

Articulate the mandatory background processes

A process is an operating system mechanism that has the ability to run a series of steps. Depending on the operating system, this may be called a job, task, or thread. Used in this context, a thread is equivalent to a process. An Oracle database instance has the following process types:

- **Client processes** – These processes run the software code for an application program or an Oracle tool.
- **Server processes** – Server processes communicate with client processes and interact with the database to fulfill requests.
- **Background processes** – Background processes consolidate functions that otherwise would require multiple Oracle Database programs running for each client process. Background processes perform I/O and monitor other Oracle Database processes.

Client Processes

When a user runs a program such as SQL*Developer or SQL*Plus, a client process (also known as a user process) is created by the operating system. Client processes interact with server processes in order to interface with the database. Server processes always run on the same machine as the Oracle database, while client processes generally run on a different machine. The client process has no direct access to the SGA of the database, but the servicing server process does. When the client process runs on the client machine, it is known as two-tier architecture. In some cases, the client process may run on an application server. This is known as a three-tiered architecture.

Server Processes

Server processes are created by the Oracle Database to handle the requests of client processes connected to the instance. A client process cannot communicate with the database on its own. It always communicates with the database through a separate server process. Server processes can perform the following tasks:

- Parse and run SQL statements
- Execute PL/SQL code
- Read data blocks from data files into the database buffer cache
- Return results from the database to the application

Mandatory Background Processes

The mandatory background processes are present in all typical database configurations. These processes run by default in a database instance started with a minimally configured initialization parameter file. Any processes that contain one or more n's can have multiple incarnations. Each version will be given successive integers (DBW0, DBW1, etc).

- **Process Monitor Process (PMON)** – As its name suggests, PMON monitors all of the other background processes. When a server or dispatcher process terminates abnormally, PMON performs process recovery. It is also responsible for cleaning up the database buffer cache and freeing resources that were allocated for client processes. PMON also registers information about the instance and dispatcher processes with the Oracle Net Listener.
- **Listener Registration Process (LREG)** -- The listener registration process (LREG) is new with the 12c release. It registers information about the database instance and dispatcher processes with the Oracle Net listener. When an instance starts, LREG polls the listener to determine whether it is running. If the

listener is running, then LREG passes it relevant parameters. If it is not running, then LREG periodically attempts to contact it.

- **System Monitor Process (SMON)** – SMON is in charge of a variety of system-level cleanup duties. The duties assigned to SMON include: performing instance recovery at instance startup if necessary; recovering any terminated transactions that were skipped during instance recovery; cleaning up unused temporary segments; and coalescing contiguous free extents within dictionary-managed tablespaces.
- **Database Writer Process (DBWn)** – DBWn processes write modified buffers in the database buffer cache to disk. All databases have at least one database writer process (DBW0). It's possible to configure additional DBWn processes to improve performance in databases with high levels of data modification. DBWn writes out to datafiles at the following times:

  - ✓ There are no free buffers.
  - ✓ Every 3 seconds
  - ✓ During a checkpoint
  - ✓ When there are too many dirty buffers
  - ✓ When the instance shuts down cleanly
  - ✓ When a tablespace changes status (i.e. is made read-only, or taken offline)
- **Log Writer Process (LGWR)** – LGWR manages the redo log buffer. LGWR writes one contiguous portion of the buffer to the online redo log. Once LGWR writes entries from the buffer to an online redo log file, server processes can copy new entries over the entries that were just written to disk. LGWR will write all redo entries that have been copied into the buffer since the last time it wrote if any of the following are true:

  - ✓ A user commits a transaction
  - ✓ An online redo log switch occurs
  - ✓ Three seconds have passed since LGWR last wrote
  - ✓ The redo log buffer is one-third full or contains 1 MB of buffered data
  - ✓ DBWn must write modified buffers to disk.
- **Checkpoint Process (CKPT)** – CKPT updates the control file and data file headers with checkpoint information and signals DBWn to write blocks to disk. Checkpoint information includes the

checkpoint position, SCN, location in online redo log to begin recovery, and other data useful to recovery operations. CKPT performs full checkpoints only at database shutdown or on request.

- **Manageability Monitor Processes (MMON and MMNL)** – MMON performs many tasks related to the Automatic Workload Repository (AWR). For example, MMON reports when a metric violates its threshold value, takes snapshots, and captures statistics value for recently modified SQL objects. The manageability monitor lite process (MMNL) writes statistics from the Active Session History (ASH) buffer in the SGA to disk.
- **Recoverer Process (RECO)** – In a distributed database, RECO resolves failures in distributed transactions. The RECO process of a node automatically connects to other databases involved in an in-doubt distributed transaction. When a connection is reestablished, RECO automatically resolves all in-doubt transactions.

Optional Background Processes

An optional background process is any background process not defined as mandatory. The majority of optional background processes are specific to tasks or features.

- **Archiver Processes (ARCn)** – ARCn copies online redo log files to offline storage after a redo log switch occurs. The ARCn processes can also collect transaction redo data and transmit it to standby databases. ARCn processes exist only when the database is in ARCHIVELOG mode and automatic archiving is enabled.
- **Job Queue Processes (CJQ0 and Jnnn)** – Job queue processes are used to run user jobs, often in batch mode. A job is a user-defined task scheduled to run one or more times. The job coordinator process (CJQ0) is automatically started and stopped as needed by Oracle. The coordinator process dynamically spawns job queue slave processes (Jnnn) to run the jobs.

- **Flashback Data Archiver Process (FBDA)** – FBDA archives historical rows of tracked tables into Flashback Data Archives. Any time a DML transaction on a tracked table commits, FBDA stores the pre-image of the rows into the Flashback Data Archive. It also keeps metadata on the current rows.
- **Space Management Coordinator Process (SMCO)** – SMCO coordinates the execution of space management tasks, such as proactive space allocation and space reclamation. SMCO dynamically spawns slave processes (Wnnn) to implement tasks.

Oracle Multitenant Architecture

Explain the benefits of multitenant architecture for database consolidation

The multitenant architecture introduced with Oracle 12c allows an Oracle database to function as a multitenant container database (CDB). A CDB can include zero, one, or many customer-created pluggable databases (PDBs). A PDB has the same capabilities and appears to Oracle Net clients as if it were a standard (non-CDB database). Every CDB has the following containers:

- **One root** -- A CDB will always have a single root container that stores Oracle-supplied metadata and common users. The root container is named CDB$ROOT.
- **One seed PDB** -- The seed PDB is a system-supplied template that is used to create new PDBs. The seed PDB is named PDB$SEED. It is not possible to add or modify objects in PDB$SEED.
- **User-created PDBs** -- A CDB can have zero, one, or many PDBs. A PDB is a user-created entity that contains the data and code required for a specific set of features. Each PDB is effectively a separate database in pre-12c terms.

Large organizations mist use hundreds of databases in their business running on different platforms and multiple physical servers. These databases might be using only a fraction of the hardware capacity of the server they are installed on. One solution is to place multiple databases on each server using virtual machines. However, in a VM configuration, the consolidated database instances do not share background processes, system and process memory, or Oracle metadata.

The Oracle Multitenant option enables you to consolidate data and code from multiple non-CDB databases without altering existing schemas or applications. Oracle guarantees that a PDB behaves the same as a non-CDB as seen from a client connecting with Oracle Net. Consolidating database using the multitenant architecture has the following benefits:

- **Cost reduction** -- By consolidating hardware and sharing database memory and files, the costs for hardware, storage, availability, and labor are reduced.
- **Easier and more rapid movement of data and code** -- A PDB can quickly be plugged into a CDB, unplugged from it, and then plugged into a different CDB.
- **Easier management and monitoring** -- The CDB administrator can attend to one physical database rather than split attention among multiple non-CDBs. Backup strategies and disaster recovery are simplified.
- **Separation of data and code** -- PDBs in a CDB maintain data and code separately. If critical data in a PDC is lost through a user error, the PDB administrator can use Oracle Flashback or point-in-time recovery to retrieve the lost data without affecting other PDBs.
- **Ease of performance tuning** -- The consolidated memory structures makes tuning much easier than if an administrator having to deal with multiple instances.
- **Fewer database patches and upgrades** -- It is easier patch or upgrade one database than multiple databases.

Create a pluggable database (PDB)

Pluggable databases can only be created within a container database, never within another PDB. There are a number of different sources for creating a PDB in a CDB, but all make use of the CREATE PLUGGABLE DATABASE SQL statement. Once created, the PDB will include a full data dictionary including metadata and internal links to system-supplied objects in the root. The different techniques for creating PDBs are:

Create a PDB from the Seed

The PDB$SEED container is a template for creating new PDBs. Te result after creating a new PDB from the seed is an 'empty' database very similar to what using the 'CREATE DATABASE' would generate for a non-CDB. The following SQL statement creates a PDB named ocpdb from the seed using Oracle Managed Files:

```
CREATE PLUGGABLE DATABASE ocpdb
 ADMIN USER ocpdba IDENTIFIED BY password;
```

Create a PDB by Cloning an Existing PDB

When cloning an existing PDB, the files associated with the source PDB are copied to a new location. The files are then associated with the new PDB. It is possible clone a PDB that is plugged into the same CDB or in a different CDB. When the PDB is in a different CDB, a database link must be provided for the remote CDB containing the PDB to be cloned. The following SQL statement clones a PDB named devpdb from the plugged-in PDB named ocpdb:

```
CREATE PLUGGABLE DATABASE devpdb FROM ocpdb;
```

Create a PDB by Plugging in an Unplugged PDB

Once unplugged from a CDB, a PDB consists of a set of data files and an XML metadata file. When a PDB is plugged in to a new CDB, the XML metadata file that describes the PDB and its files is used to associate the PDB with the CDB. The following SQL statement plugs in a PDB named testingpdb based on the metadata stored in the named XML file. The NOCOPY keyword is specified because the files of the unplugged PDB do not need to be renamed:

```
CREATE PLUGGABLE DATABASE testingpdb
USING '/u01/usr/testingpdb.xml' NOCOPY
```

Create a PDB from a Non-CDB

There are three basic techniques to create a PDB from an existing non-CDB. Two of them require that a blank PDB be created using the seed. Once created, GoldenGate Replication or the Oracle Data Pump utility can be used to populate the new PDB with data from the non-CDB database. The third is a more direct option that effectively makes the non-CDB look like an unplugged PDB. The database must be placed into a transactionally consistent state. Then the DBMS_PDB.DESCRIBE function is executed against the non-CDB to generate XML metadata about it. The database can then be plugged in via the same steps as the prior section for an unplugged PDB.

Articulate the difference between a Container database and a Pluggable database

In a literal sense, the 'Container Database' is everything in a multitenant installation of Oracle, the root container, the seed PDB, and all of the PDBs. However, in this context, Oracle University is presumably referring to the difference between the root container and the PDB containers. Each container (Root or PDB) is a collection of schemas, objects, and related structures. Each appears logically as a separate database and has a unique ID and name within the CDB.

- **Root** -- The root container, named CDB$ROOT, is a collection of schemas, schema objects, and nonschema objects to which all PDBs belong. There is only one root container in a given CDB and it stores the system metadata required to manage PDBs. All of the PDBs in the container database belong to the root. No user data should ever be stored in the root and the system-supplied schemas in it should never be altered. It is possible, however, to create common users and roles for database administration in the root. A common user with the necessary privileges can switch between PDBs and a common role can be granted in multiple PDBs.
- **PDB** -- Pluggable Databases are a user-created set of schemas, objects, and related structures. Each PDB appears logically to an application as a separate database. Every PDB is owned by the SYS user regardless of which user actually created the PDB. The SYS user (despite not having a name that starts with C##) is a common user in the CDB.

Perform administration tasks on a container database (CDB)

The administration tasks for a CDB are, for the most part, the same as for a non-CDB. Where there are differences, it is usually because of their scope. Some administrative tasks are applicable to the entire CDB, some only to the root, and some to individual pluggable databases (PDBs). This chapter describes how to complete these tasks. Oracle 12c has specific roles for CDB administrators vs. PDB administrators (CDB_DBA and PDB_DBA respectively).

The data dictionary for each container in a CDB is fully separate from the other containers. The 'current container' is the one whose data dictionary is being used for name resolution and for privilege authorization. The current container can be the root or a PDB. A session can have only one current container at any point in time. However, for accounts with access to multiple containers, it is possible for a session to switch from one to another.

The SYS_CONTEXT function can be called with the CON_ID or CON_NAME parameters in the USERENV namespace to determine the current container ID or name with. The following query returns the current container name:

```
SELECT SYS_CONTEXT('USERENV', 'CON_NAME') FROM dual;
```

Some items to note about administering a CDB include:

- Only common users can have CDB$ROOT as the current container. Local users cannot access the root. A given PDB can be the current container for both common users and local users. When executing a SQL statement that includes CONTAINER = ALL, the current container must be the root and the user must have the commonly granted SET CONTAINER privilege.
- Common users perform administrative tasks for a CDB. Some tasks, such as starting up a CDB instance, can only be performed by a common user.

- There is only one alert log for the entire CDB. The name of a PDB is included in records in trace files, when appropriate.

Common vs. Local Users

The 12c Multitenant Architecture has introduced the concept of common and local users. A common user is a database user that has the same identity in the root and in every existing and future PDB. Common users can connect to and perform operations within the root, and within any PDB in which it has been granted privileges. A user connected to the root can perform certain operations, such as ALTER PLUGGABLE DATABASE, CREATE USER, CREATE ROLE, that affect other pluggable databases (PDBs). However, most privileges can only be exercised within the current container. Users must first switch to the PDB where the action is to be taken, and then exercise their privileges from there. For example, a common user cannot query tables or views in a PDB when it is not the current container.

Creating a common user account:

- You must be connected to the root and have the commonly granted CREATE USER system privilege.
- The session's current container must be CDB$ROOT.
- The name of the common user must start with C## or c## and contain only ASCII or EDCDIC characters.
- To explicitly designate a user account as a common user, in the CREATE USER statement, specify CONTAINER=ALL. When logged into the root, if the CONTAINER clause is omitted, CONTAINER=ALL is implied.

No objects should be created in the schemas of common users. They cannot be shared across PDB boundaries and can cause problems during plug-in and unplug operations. Schema objects owned by Oracle-created common users are shared throughout the entire CDB. The following example creates a common user account and grants the user the SET

CONTAINER and CREATE SESSION privileges (common users must have these privileges to navigate between containers):

```
CREATE USER c##ocp_admin
  IDENTIFIED BY password
  DEFAULT TABLESPACE ts_cdb_users
  QUOTA 100M ON ts_cdb_users
  TEMPORARY TABLESPACE temp_ts
  CONTAINER = ALL;
GRANT SET CONTAINER, CREATE SESSION TO c##ocp_admin CONTAINER = ALL;
```

Creating a local user account:

Local user accounts exist only in the PDB that they are created in. They cannot connect to or be granted privileges in other PDBs. It is possible, of course, to create a user of the same name in multiple PDBs, but the accounts share nothing except the name. To create a local user account:

- You must be connected to the PDB in which you want to create the account, and have the CREATE USER privilege.
- The name of the local user must not start with C## or c##.
- The clause CONTAINER=CURRENT can be included in the CREATE USER statement to explicitly specify the user as a local user. When connected to a PDB, if the clause is omitted, CONTAINER=CURRENT is implied.

```
CREATE USER ocp_user
  IDENTIFIED BY password
  DEFAULT TABLESPACE ts_pdb_users
  QUOTA 100M ON ts_pdb_users
  TEMPORARY TABLESPACE temp_ts
  PROFILE ocp_profile
  CONTAINER = CURRENT;
```

While a common user can create a local user by specifying the PDB in the CONTAINER clause, a local user cannot create a common user. Common users can only be created when CDB$ROOT is the current container and a local user cannot create a session in the root.

Privileges and Roles in a CDB

When using the Multitenant option, privileges and roles (like users) can be either common or local. Common users and local users can grant privileges to one another. A given privilege (i.e. CREATE ANY TABLE) is neither common nor local by itself. If CREATE ANY TABLE is granted commonly, then it becomes a common privilege, and if granted locally, it becomes a local privilege.

Commonly granted privileges:

- A privilege that is granted commonly can be used in every existing and future container.
- Only common users can grant privileges commonly, and only to a common user or common role.
- The grantor must be connected to the root and must specify CONTAINER=ALL in the GRANT statement.
- Can include system and object privileges.
- Should never be granted to PUBLIC.

Locally granted privileges:

- A privilege granted locally can be used only in the container in which it was granted, even when granted in the root.
- Both common users and local users can grant privileges locally.
- A common user and a local user can grant privileges to other common or local roles.
- The grantor must be connected to the container and must specify CONTAINER=CURRENT in the GRANT statement.
- Any user can grant a privilege locally to any other user or role (both common and local) or to the PUBLIC role.

The CONTAINER clause in a GRANT or REVOKE statement determines where a privilege is granted to or revoked from. When the CONTAINER is set to ALL, the statement applies the privilege to all existing and future containers. Using CURRENT in the clause will apply the privilege to the local container. The value will default to CURRENT if the clause is omitted except when connected to the root, when the default will be ALL. The following example grants the CREATE TABLE privilege to common user c##ocp_admin. After the grant, the user will be able to use the privilege in all existing and future containers.

```
GRANT CREATE TABLE TO c##ocp_admin CONTAINER=ALL;
```

Common roles are created in the root and are known in all existing and future containers. All Oracle-supplied predefined roles are common roles. Local roles exist in only the PDB they were created in and can only be used there. Local roles cannot have any commonly granted privileges.

- Common users can both create and grant common roles to other common and local users.
- A common role can be granted to a common user either commonly or locally.
- If a common role is granted to a local user, the privileges from the role apply only to the local user's PDB.
- Local users cannot create common roles
- Local users can grant common roles to common and local users.

If the following requirements are met, commonly granted privileges that have been made to a common role apply in the root and all current and future PDBs to which the grantor can connect:

- Both the grantor and the grantee are common users.
- The grantor possesses the commonly granted SET CONTAINER privilege and the ADMIN OPTION for the common role.
- The GRANT statement contains the CONTAINER=ALL clause.

The name given to user-created common roles must start with C## or c## and contain only ASCII or EDCDIC characters (this does not apply to Oracle-supplied roles, such as DBA or RESOURCE). When the role is created, the CONTAINER clause must be set to ALL. Except when logged in to the root, omitting this clause from the CREATE ROLE statement creates a local role in the current PDB. If the CONTAINER clause is omitted when logged in to the root, by default the role is created as a common role. The following example creates the c##ocp_mgr common role:

```
CREATE ROLE c##ocp_admin CONTAINER=ALL;
```

Manage processes in a CDB

A CDB has one instance and one set of background processes shared by the root and all PDBs. A single system global area (SGA) and a single aggregate program global area (PGA) is allocated for the entire CDB. The memory required by a container database is the sum of the memory requirements for all of the PDBs that will be part of it.

The task of managing the processes is effectively identical to that of a non-CDB. The instance and process structure of Oracle were discussed in an earlier chapter.

Manage physical and logical structures in a CDB

A tablespace is a logical storage container for database objects that consume storage space. At the physical level, a tablespace consists of one or more operating system files. Tablespaces in a CDB have the following characteristics:

- A permanent tablespace can be associated with only one container.
- Tablespaces are associated only with the container they are created in.
- A CDB has a single active undo tablespace or one active undo tablespace for each instance of an Oracle RAC CDB.

- The root has a set of Oracle-supplied tablespaces, such as the SYSTEM tablespace. Each PDB has its own set of Oracle-supplied tablespaces.
- The root has its own data files, and each PDB has its own data files.
- There is a default temporary tablespace for the entire CDB. PDBs can use the default or optionally additional temporary tablespaces can be created for use by individual PDBs.
- Each container in a CDB must have its own default permanent tablespace. Users connected to the container who are not explicitly assigned a tablespace use the container's default permanent tablespace.

Describe the various storage options for a PDB

Each PDB has its own data files that can be managed in the same way that as a non-CDB. It is possible to limit the amount of storage used by the data files for a PDB by using the STORAGE clause in a CREATE PLUGGABLE DATABASE or ALTER PLUGGABLE DATABASE statement. The STORAGE clause can be used to specify the following limits:

- The MAXSIZE keyword is used to set the amount of storage that can be used by all tablespaces that belong to the PDB:

```
STORAGE (MAXSIZE 20G)
```

- The MAX_SHARED_TEMP_SIZE sets the amount of storage in the default temporary tablespace shared by all PDBs that can be used by sessions connected to the PDB"

```
STORAGE (MAX_SHARED_TEMP_SIZE 200M)
```

If the STORAGE clause is left off, or the values are explicitly set to UNLIMITED, then there are no storage limits set on the space used by the PDB.

Oracle Network Architecture

Describe the differences between Shared Server and Dedicated Server architecture as it relates to Oracle Connection Manager

The Oracle Connection Manager is a proxy server that forwards connection requests to databases or other proxy servers. It usually resides on a computer separate from the database server and client computers. The primary functions of Oracle Connection Manager are:

- **Access control** -- To use rule-based configuration to filter user-specified client requests and accept others.
- **Session multiplexing** -- To funnel multiple client sessions through a network connection to a shared server destination.

Oracle's shared server architecture is designed to be used in environments with very high numbers of client connections. In cases where client load causes a strain on memory and other system resources, using shared server resources can help. When utilizing the shared server architecture, the database allows multiple client processes to share a small number of server processes. The number of users that can be supported is significantly increased. When enabled, many client processes connect to a dispatcher and it directs incoming network session requests to a common queue. An idle shared server process from a shared pool picks up a request from the queue.

Session multiplexing enables multiple client sessions to funnel through a single protocol connection. Oracle Connection Manager allows communication by users to the dispatcher by way of a shared connection. Session multiplexing is beneficial because it maximizes use of the dispatcher process connections. Session multiplexing is enabled by setting the MULTIPLEX attribute in the DISPATCHERS parameter to 'on' or an equivalent value.

```
DISPATCHERS="(PROTOCOL=tcp)(MULTIPLEX=on)"
```

Describe the Oracle Database listener architecture

Oracle Net Services is the element that provides connectivity solutions in distributed computing environments. One component of Oracle Net Services, Oracle Net, enables a network session from a client application to an Oracle Database server. Any time a network session is established between a client application and the database, Oracle Net acts as the data courier. It establishes and maintains the connection between the client application and the database. Throughout the life of the session it is integral in exchanging messages between them. Oracle Net enables connections from traditional client/server applications to Oracle Database servers. Oracle Net resides on both the client and the database server and communicates with TCP/IP to facilitate connectivity and data transfer between the client and the database. The graphic below shows how Oracle Net enables a network connection between a client and a database server.

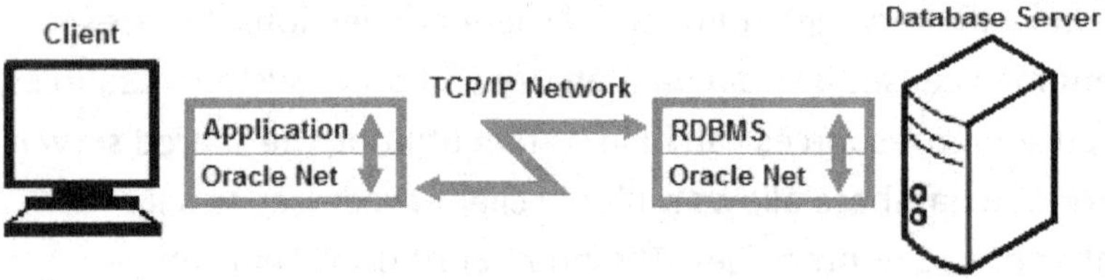

Figure 3: Oracle Net client-server connection

On the client computer, Oracle Net is a background component that facilitates application connections to the database. On the server side, the Oracle Net Listener coordinates connections between the database and client connections. While the most common use of Oracle Net Services is to handle incoming Oracle database connections, it can also be used as an interface to non Oracle data sources (such as SQL Server and DB2) or to access external code libraries via EXTPROC.

The Oracle Database server receives the initial connection through Oracle Net Listener (referred to henceforth as the listener). The listener is an Oracle background process that listens on a specific port for database connection requests. It brokers a client request and hands off the request to the server. The listener is configured with a protocol address. Clients configured to use that protocol address can send connection requests to the listener. Once a connection has been established, the client and Oracle server communicate directly with one another. Stopping the listener will prevent new connections from occurring, but will not affect existing connections.

When the database is in a dedicated server configuration, the listener starts a separate dedicated server process for each incoming client connection. The server process thus created is dedicated to servicing the one client. When the session is complete, the dedicated server process terminates. The steps for the listener passing a client connection request to a dedicated server process and the establishment of a database session follow:

1. The listener receives a client connection request.
2. The listener starts a dedicated server process, and the dedicated server inherits the connection request from the listener.
3. The client is now connected directly to the dedicated server.
4. The server process checks the client's authentication credentials.
5. If credentials are valid, a session to the database is created.

Configure and connect to a database service

In order to connect to a database service, clients must use a connect descriptor that provides both the location of the database and the name of the database service. The following example is an Easy Connect descriptor that connects to a database service named ocp.exam.com, and the host ocp-server (by default the port that will be used is 1521): ocp-server/ocp.exam.com

In order for the above connection to work, the database being connected to must have a matching entry in the configuration file tnsnames.ora. The matching entry in that file for the preceding connect descriptor and database service would be:

```
(DESCRIPTION=
(ADDRESS=(PROTOCOL=tcp)(HOST=ocp-server)(PORT=1521))
(CONNECT_DATA=
(SERVICE_NAME=ocp.exam.com)))
```

A connect descriptor is a specially formatted description of the destination for a network connection. It contains the destination service and network route information. The destination service is indicated by name and the network route by the location of the listener through the use of a network address. A connect descriptor is comprised of one or more protocol addresses of the listener and the connect information for the destination service in the tnsnames.ora file. The below example is a connect descriptor for the ocp database.

```
ocp=
(DESCRIPTION=
      (ADDRESS=(PROTOCOL=tcp)
                 (HOST=ocp-server)
                 (PORT=1521)
      )
      (CONNECT_DATA=(SID=ocp)
                      (SERVICE_NAME=ocp.exam.com)
                      (INSTANCE_NAME=ocp)
      )
)
```

The ADDRESS section contains the following parameters:

- **PROTOCOL** – Identifies the listener protocol address. The protocol 'tcp' is used for TCP/IP.
- **HOST** – Identifies the host name. The host is ocp-server. You can also use an IP address when using the TCP/IP protocol.
- **PORT** – Identifies the port. 1521 is the default port used by Oracle Net.

The CONNECT_DATA section contains the following parameters:

- **SID** – Identifies the SID of the Oracle database. In this case the SID is ocp.
- **SERVICE_NAME** – Identifies the service. The destination service name is a database service named ocp.exam.com. The value for this parameter comes from the SERVICE_NAMES initialization parameter. Generally the SERVICE_NAMES parameter is the global database name.
- **INSTANCE_NAME** – Identifies the database instance. This parameter is optional and defaults to the SID entered during installation or database creation.

Configure a database listener

The Oracle Installer launches the Oracle Net Configuration Assistant during installation. The Net Configuration Assistant automatically configures the listening protocol address and service information for Oracle Database. During a standard installation, the listener is automatically configured with a name of LISTENER that has a TCP/IP listening protocol address for Oracle Database. If a Custom installation is used, the Net Configuration Assistant will prompt for the listener name and protocol address. Regardless of the installation type, a listening IPC protocol address for external procedure calls is automatically configured. Service information for the external procedures is also configured automatically in the listener.ora file.

If the current configuration is not adequate for a particular environment, the Oracle Net Manager can be used to customize the listener.ora configuration. The steps for doing so are:

- Start Oracle Net Manager.
- In the navigator pane, expand Local, and then select Listeners.
- Select the listener.
- From the list in the right pane, select Listener Locations.
- Select the protocol from the Protocol list.
- Enter the host name for the listener in the Host field.
- Enter the port number in the Port field.
- If you want to set send and receive buffer sizes, then click Show Advanced, and then enter the sizes in the appropriate fields.
- Select Save Network Configuration from the File menu to save the changes.

ABOUT THE AUTHOR

Matthew Morris is an Oracle Database Administrator and Developer currently employed as a Database Engineer with Computer Sciences Corporation. Matthew has worked with the Oracle database since 1996 when he worked in the RDBMS support team for Oracle Support Services. Employed with Oracle for over eleven years in support and development positions, Matthew was an early adopter of the Oracle Certified Professional program. He was one of the first one hundred Oracle Certified Database Administrators (version 7.3) and in the first hundred to become an Oracle Certified Forms Developer. In the years since, he has upgraded his Database Administrator certification for releases 8i, 9i, 10G and 11G, become an Oracle Advanced PL/SQL Developer Certified Professional and added the Expert certifications for Application Express, SQL, and SQL Tuning.

Made in the USA
Monee, IL
04 November 2026

67383582R00105